SO-ARJ-145

Designing
Your Practice

Designing Your Practice

A Principal's Guide
to Creating and Managing
a Design Practice

Norman Kaderlan

McGraw-Hill, Inc.

New York   St. Louis   San Francisco   Auckland   Bogotá
Caracas   Hamburg   Lisbon   London   Madrid
Mexico   Milan   Montreal   New Delhi   Paris
San Juan   São Paulo   Singapore
Sydney   Tokyo   Toronto

Library of Congress Cataloging-in-Publication Data

Kaderlan, Norman S.
  Designing your practice / Norman Kaderlan.
     p.   cm.
  Includes index.
  ISBN 0-07-033254-1
  1. Architectural practice — United States — Management.   I. Title.
  NA1996.K3   1991
  720'.68 — dc20   90-49755
                                                                          CIP

Copyright © 1991 by McGraw-Hill, Inc. All rights reserved. Printed in the United States of America. Except as permitted under the United States Copyright Act of 1976, no part of this publication may be reproduced or distributed in any form or by any means, or stored in a data base or retrieval system, without the prior written permission of the publisher.

1 2 3 4 5 6 7 8 9 0   DOC/DOC   9 6 5 4 3 2 1 0

ISBN   0-07-033254-1

The sponsoring editor for this book was Joel Stein, the editing supervisor was Kimberly A. Goff, and the production supervisor was Pamela A. Pelton. This book was set in Baskerville. It was composed by McGraw-Hill's Professional Publishing composition unit.

Printed and bound by R. R. Donnelley & Sons Company.

To Louise:
Who spurred me on and saw me through

Contents

Part 3. Making It Happen

Appendix B. Alternative Planning Techniques   177

Preface

When looking through the literature of design practice management, one finds little to help a principal translate his or her vision into an organizational framework. There is, however, a rich source of ideas and techniques in the literature of management and organizational behavior. These models and methods represent the essence of people's experiences of what successful managers do and unsuccessful ones don't do. The problem is that most design professionals are not familiar with this knowledge; it is difficult for them to understand how such ideas can relate to their situations.

This book bridges the gap between current management thought and management practice in design. It presents concepts of management and organizations and shows how they can be adapted to the unique circumstances of a design practice. When appropriately applied these techniques can help principals design their practices to be more effective in achieving their goals.

The idea for *Designing Your Practice* came to me 3 years ago. To gather material for the book, I interviewed 45 principals of design firms — architects, interior designers, landscape architects — about how they determined success for themselves and for their practice. The results were paradoxical. The principals saw their practice as the instrument through which they achieve professional goals, but they focus most of their energy and attention on individual projects. They saw the practice as a progression of projects rather than as a whole.

The paradox was caused by the lack of a practice perspective. One way to achieve such a perspective is to treat the creation and development of the practice as a design problem. There are many parallels between designing a project and designing a practice. The processes of design, planning, decision making, and problem solving are all analogous even though the media the processes use and the environment within which they occur may differ. The same method that an architect or interior designer uses to design a building or a space can be used to design a practice. Although architects and interior designers may lack formal training in management and business, they already have some of the basic concepts.

The experience of managing a wide range of creative activities and organizations for 20 years has contributed to my understanding of designers and the design process. In researching this book, I interviewed more than 100 principals and staff members of design firms ranging in size from 1 to 700 employees. The interviews provided illustrations of what to do and what to avoid. All the examples cited in the text are the experiences of actual firms. However, in some cases I have used the firm's initials or left quotes unattributed to preserve the anonymity of the source.

I would like to acknowledge those who assisted me throughout this project. I am grateful to Jody Greenwald, director of the Interior and Environmental Design Program at the University of California at Los Angeles Extension for giving me the opportunity to develop the course that launched this project; to Joel Stein, who first suggested the idea of a book based upon these principles; to Andrea Henninger, who collaborated with me on the study of success; and to the members of the Principal's Roundtable of the Los Angeles Chapter of the Institute of Business Designers as well as the other individuals who participated in the interviews.

I am also grateful to my sister, Louise Kaderlan, and Martha Drexler Lynn for their assistance, support, and encouragement; to Mackey Deasy for his comments and helpful suggestions; and to my son, Joshua, who put up with his Dad's crazy work schedule.

Norman Kaderlan

1
Introduction

Your vision defines your practice. As the buildings and spaces you create are a reflection of you, so is your practice.

As principal, you set the standard for the practice. You define its goals and shape its values. You are the model for staff and clients. Your goals, values, and philosophy become the goals, values, and philosophy of the practice.

The purpose of the practice is to carry out your goals. To the extent that the practice attains those goals, you are successful.

Success is an elusive quality, difficult to define. Design professionals measure success in very personal ways. A 1987 study examined how principals of design firms determine whether they are successful.[1] The subjects used 100 different factors, only two of which were mentioned by more than a majority: (1) having a continuing source of work coming from satisfied clients through repeat work and referrals and (2) having the respect of colleagues, as measured by awards, honors, and publications. Other factors, mentioned by fewer than half of those interviewed, included the quality of design, financial rewards, self-satisfaction, having good projects and good clients, independence and autonomy, and having a profitable firm.

The variation in those factors—and the lack of consensus—suggests that design professionals judge success individually: in terms of their own aims, values, and preferences. There are no universal professional standards. Rather, success is the attainment of personal professional goals.

The study did find consensus on one point. Without exception, the

---

[1] The study, conducted by the author and Andrea Henninger, consisted of interviews of 45 principals of design firms in southern California. The subjects were asked how they determined success for themselves and for their practice.

1

principals saw no difference between the success of their practices and their own success. Their practices were the mechanisms through which they achieved their personal goals as design professionals.

You can define success any way you wish. Your standards can be objective or subjective, internal or external. They can be aesthetic, financial, personal, or organizational. However you define them, they become the design criteria for your practice.

There are many ways in which designing a practice is comparable to designing a building or space. Mel Hamilton, design partner of ISD Interiors, sees the two as similar:

> I think you approach the design of the practice with the same kind of problem solving that you use in a project. You define what you want and need and get the right kind of people.

You have a powerful tool to use in this effort. As a formal method of creative problem solving, the design process provides a systematic approach to almost any kind of problem. You already know how to apply this method to the design of a building or an interior space. This book explores how the same technique can be applied to the design of a practice.

Each of the elements involved in designing a building has a counterpart in the design of a practice. As a designer creating a building or space, you work with the client, the program, the users, the site, a budget, and materials. As a principal creating your practice, you are both the client and the designer. You are the client because the organization is created to carry out your goals. You are the designer because you are the one who conceives and shapes the practice.

The market environment in which the practice exists is the equivalent of the project site. The program for the practice is determined by a combination of your goals and the needs of the marketplace. Project clients are the users of the practice, since the practice serves their needs through the services it provides. The money a practice has available to finance its activities serves the same function as a project budget. The people in the practice are the materials, the building blocks of the organization.

The major difference between designing a building and crafting a practice is the nature of the environment, both external and internal. With a building, the site is a constant and the materials have known and predictable characteristics. Once the project is built, the results are literally cast in concrete.

The practice, on the other hand, exists in a dynamic external environment. Business and marketing conditions are constantly changing; they expose the firm to forces over which it has no control. The state of the economy, the needs of the clients, and the regulatory environment are in constant flux.

Internally, the environment of the practice also is dynamic. Unlike building materials, whose characteristics are known and predictable, the needs, desires, and attitudes of people on staff are never constant or static. As the firm grows, as new employees come on staff, the mix of people's needs changes; in changing, it transforms the nature of the practice. The volatility of the environment requires that the practice be continually recreated. What works today may not work six months from now; what didn't work yesterday may well work tomorrow.

Ignoring changing circumstances puts a practice at risk. When a California architectural practice grew from 12 to 45 people in a year, the principals initially tried to manage the expanded firm in the same way they operated the smaller one. It didn't work. The principals put in twice as many hours, had half as much fun, and lost money. Only after 2 years of great difficulty did they recognize that they had to change. They found out the hard way that old solutions don't always apply to new circumstances.

To create a practice, talent is not enough. Many skills and abilities play important parts in achieving your goals. Three elements in particular contribute to success: vision, leadership, and acumen. *Vision* is a clear sense of your goals based on a central core of deeply held values. Goals and values give purpose to the practice, provide a sense of direction, and act as a moral compass. Without clear goals, the practice has no direction.

Three Elements of Success

Vision A clear sense of your goals based on a central core of deeply held values.

Leadership The ability to marshal the necessary resources, talents, and abilities—yours and those of others—to act on your vision.

Acumen The ability to make decisions that reconcile difficult choices with contradictory goals.

Leadership transforms vision into reality. Vision is the basis of action, but by itself it is not sufficient. It must be translated into performance. Leadership is the ability to marshal the necessary resources, talents, and abilities—yours and those of others—to act on the vision.

Acumen is the ability to make decisions that reconcile difficult choices among goals that are often contradictory. Rarely is the path to a goal clear and straightforward. Most often, your choices are alternatives whose consequences conflict, options that are equally undesirable, or possibilities the implications of which are not clear. Acumen is the skill to evaluate the tradeoffs and to know when it is necessary to give in and when to hold firm. Acumen is also the capacity to make decisions under conditions of uncertainty and ambiguity.

The foundation on which those skills are based is the perspective that a practice is more than a succession of projects. It is the framework within which projects are produced. It provides the resources for projects and a supportive environment in which the project process can take place.

This perspective includes the systematic and constructive use of experience. The successful firm learns from its experience in two ways. It learns how to do things better so it doesn't repeat the same mistakes. It learns how to do things differently so the entire process can be improved. The skills for designing your practice can be learned. In the chapters that follow, ideas and practical tools for their development and use are presented.

Part 1 discusses the skills needed for setting a direction. The first step in designing the practice is to define your vision. You do that by developing a plan for your practice, just as you develop a plan for a building or an interior space. Chapter 2 shows how planning your practice demands the same techniques as the design process. It describes a new approach to planning that is more compatible with the way design professionals work than traditional approaches. It outlines in detail the steps involved in creating a plan for your practice.

The collaborative nature of architecture and interior design requires you to work with and through other people to achieve your vision. Chapter 3 discusses a number of ideas about leadership and management. You will learn specific strategies as well as suggestions for developing your leadership skills. Those ideas will help you decide what leadership style is appropriate for your practice.

Part 2 discusses specific design strategies that are useful in carrying out your vision. The structure of an organization functions like a program for the practice: It defines relationships, responsibilities, flow of work, and the way work gets done. Chapter 4 discusses several frameworks you can use to analyze your practice and describes how they can help you choose the appropriate structure. It shows you why certain structures work in specific situations. It also describes how needs change as the practice grows and evolves.

Chapter 5 deals with managing people, the practice's most important resource. It shows how you can match people to the practice and get the most out of them by properly recruiting, motivating, and rewarding employees.

Satisfied clients are the most effective marketing tool you have. They also make your work less risky and more enjoyable than difficult clients do. In Chapter 6, you will learn what you can do to make the relationship with your client a positive one.

Designers are constantly working in and with groups: project teams, studios, staffs, committees, departments, and task forces. A small office is also a group. Chapter 7 discusses how groups grow and the issues with which every group must deal. It describes specific suggestions for making them more effective. It also discusses how to make better decisions. It concludes with a model for deciding when to make decisions yourself and when to involve the group.

Part 3 discusses how to implement the design for your practice. Chapter 8 describes ways to increase personal effectiveness. It presents principles, tools, and techniques for linking daily activities with longer-range goals.

As your practice grows and evolves, it creates a history as well as a future. Chapter 9 deals with organizational learning and change. Learning makes it possible to do things better as well as to do better things. The chapter concludes with a discussion of how to manage the change that is the inevitable result of learning.

Your understanding of the design process combined with these skills will enable you to practice by design. The challenge is to apply a familiar process to an unfamiliar context. Dan Dworsky, of Dan Dworsky and Associates, put it best:

> To solve a management puzzle takes the same kind of effort, the same kind of skill, and can provide for the same kind of creativity as solving a design puzzle. It's not as easy because it's not as natural. But you have to accept that responsibility.

PART 1
Setting the Direction

2

Vision and Planning

If you don't know where you're going, you'll probably end up somewhere else. YOGI BERRA

Clear vision is essential in the design of your practice. It focuses your attention on what is important. Your vision energizes the practice and defines its direction. But vision by itself is not enough. It must be spelled out so that others can understand it, buy into it, help make it happen. When designing a building or an interior, you communicate your vision through working drawings. When designing a practice, you express your vision through a strategic plan.

The Benefits of Planning

Through planning, you get in touch with what really matters. That was the experience of SRA, a contract interior design firm in southern California. Since its founding 30 years ago, the firm had changed direction several times in response to pressures of competition and the marketplace. Four years ago, the principals realized that they had lost sight of what was important to them. The enjoyment and satisfaction had faded.

To recapture their vision, the two principals began to plan. They started by reexamining their values, and they found that the practice's mission was not fulfilling those values. What really mattered to them was the quality of their designs, but the practice did not pursue that purpose. They changed the firm's mission and modified their strategy to concentrate on clients who appreciated and could pay for excellent design.

As a result, both the personal and professional rewards to the princi-

9

pals increased substantially. This, according to one of the principals, was the lesson:

> The key to our survival was our ability to communicate with ourselves, to understand what is really meaningful and rewarding to us. We had to ask: "What are we good at? What do we enjoy?" Our history has been a search for our core values, our goals.

Planning empowers you to create your future.[1] Though you cannot control external events, you can control your actions. By acting with purpose, you can create situations that will let you fulfill that purpose. Planning is a way of being proactive with your practice and accepting responsibility for your future. Planning is a way to look at the future in terms of the present.

Your mission and goals are like magnets, pulling your practice toward them. They shape your actions by defining appropriate courses of action. You now have a benchmark for making decisions. When faced with a choice you can ask: Which option moves me closer to my goal? Which alternative is more in line with my mission? SRA's new mission was a vision of the future that reoriented the entire practice. Its plan outlined the actions it needed to take in order to meet that mission.

When you plan, you establish priorities for your practice. Using these priorities as guides, you can concentrate on the activities that provide the greatest progress toward your goals. That allows you to get the most from such limited resources as time, energy, and money. By acting on your priorities, which are based on your goals, you establish a link between what you do today and what you want for the future. As that connection becomes clear, it acts as a powerful motivating force.

Planning also provides a context for decision making. Your mission, goals, and strategies become design criteria by which you evaluate alternatives. When you have to decide about an opportunity you can ask how it fits with the plan. If it fits, you can proceed; if it doesn't fit, you have two options: You can decide not to go forward or you can revise your plan in light of the unanticipated opportunity. The plan gives you a framework within which you can consider your actions, no matter which way you proceed.

To illustrate how a plan helps in making decisions, consider the situation of a midsize architectural firm the two principals of which developed a plan for their practice last year. Though the firm is a general practice, most of its recent projects have been residences and restaurants from a particular franchise. Through their planning process, the

---

[1] For a fuller discussion of the benefits of strategic planning, see George A. Steiner, *Strategic Planning*, The Free Press, New York, 1979.

principals decided not to do any more restaurants; they preferred to concentrate on commercial work instead.

Four months after they finished the plan, a client asked them to design a restaurant. How did they use the plan to make their decision?

If the project had been a house or apartment building, there would have been no question about taking it; the opportunity would have been completely in line with their goals. Though the project was not consistent with their plan, the principals still had a choice. They could stick by their plan and decide not to take the offer, or they could take the project.

The reason for turning the project down was that the project would hinder progress toward their goals rather than help it. On the other hand, there could have been at least two reasons for pursuing the project: Short-term goals such as cash flow or survival might take precedence over longer-term goals, or the project might offer an opportunity they hadn't anticipated when they put their plan together. That opportunity could have been so attractive they might have been willing to reconsider their plan. In that situation, there was no "right" decision. Any decision can be appropriate as long as it is considered within the context of the plan.

Planning saves time. It enables you to anticipate developments before they occur. You can prepare contingencies ahead of time instead of in the middle of a crisis. Because planning gives you ways to deal with the expected, you have more time to deal with the unexpected. You also have more time to be creative.

Planning aids organizational memory. By comparing performance with projection, you can learn from experience. For example, by reviewing data on the number and types of changes in construction drawings that are due to errors and omissions, you might find clues to improving the process itself. Analyzing your experience in meeting project budgets will help you to do a better job of estimating project costs in the future.

Planning requires that you adopt a practice perspective. In developing your plan, you must consider the practice as a whole and examine the interaction among its components. You need to understand the effect of an action in one part of the practice on the other parts. If your plan calls for an expanded marketing effort, for example, you also need to provide a way to handle the increased work load that will result.

Planning is a process that allows you to adapt continually to a dynamic environment. The plan is your best estimate of what can and should be done to achieve your goals under a given set of circumstances. Because circumstances can and do change, you must be prepared to adjust the plan accordingly. The process of planning is as important as the plan itself.

The product of the process is the plan. The plan is a blueprint for action. Like a set of drawings for an interior space, a plan should communicate your intent to those who have to implement it. A clear plan allows the staff to concentrate on achieving its goals instead of wasting time figuring out what is expected of it. Properly done, planning improves staff morale and increases productivity and effectiveness.

Planning gives people a way to gauge their performances; goals and objectives provide yardsticks by which staff members can measure their achievement. That helps them keep on track and motivated.

Why People Resist Planning

There are several reasons why principals don't plan. First, and most prevalent, is fear of failure. A plan puts the principal on record about what he or she wants to accomplish and holds him or her accountable if the goals are not reached. For many people, that can be a very threatening situation. It exposes them to feelings of vulnerability and loss of self-esteem. They prefer not to have clear standards for their performance — that way, they don't risk failure.

Fear of success is a second reason for not planning. Some people are afraid that if they succeed in meeting their goals, they will be expected to do even better the next time. They will be trapped in a spiral of higher expectations and greater pressures, and that is too great a burden for them to handle. So they don't even try.

Many design professionals don't plan because they feel that the planning process is unsuited to their temperament. Some creative individuals think that planning restricts their ability to respond to a situation spontaneously. Planning, they feel, requires them to know what they want ahead of time. They don't want to be pinned down because they don't know where their creativity will take them.

Those fears arise from a traditional approach to planning that emphasizes the result over the process. In that view, the plan is the thing. It assumes that you know what you want to do before you can go out and do it. You clarify your goals by using logic, analysis, and rationality. Goals are set from above. By selecting specific goals at the outset, you can focus your thinking and concentrate your resources on only the things that are important. Once goals are determined, the entire organization is committed to their achievement.

A drawback of the traditional approach is its emphasis on the plan as opposed to the process. Because the firm has invested so heavily in it, people are reluctant to change the plan, even in the face of a changing environment. Making the plan becomes the most important goal. Anything that doesn't fit the plan is ignored or swept aside. That attitude prevents the practice from learning from its experience and adjusting to a dynamic environment.

The traditional approach is very efficient for those who have a clear idea of exactly what they want, those who can set their direction by using analytical methods. However, not everyone in the design professions operates in that manner. Many design professionals don't always know exactly what they want to do. They may prefer to explore and experiment within a general direction and see where it leads them. They would rather act first and figure it out later.

For people who operate this way, there is another approach, *emergent planning*.[2] It recognizes that people don't always know why they act in a certain way. Whenever they do act, however, it is with a purpose, even if they don't always know what that purpose is. In emergent planning, if you don't know exactly what you do want, you can plan for what you don't want. By saying what you don't want to do, you create boundaries within which you can do anything. Inside those boundaries, you can freely explore, experiment, and develop a variety of approaches. After a period, you can look back at your actions to see what worked and what patterns emerged. You can then examine the patterns to see what purpose they reflect. When your actions converge into meaningful patterns, your mission emerges.

The case of SRA illustrates how emergent planning works. Over most of the history of the firm, the principals did not have a clearly defined mission. When they eventually evaluated their experience, they discovered that the projects that allowed them to pursue design excellence were the ones that were most successful and rewarding. Out of that pattern came their mission to focus on high-quality design.

The Design Process and Strategic Planning

Strategic planning is the application of the design process to your practice. The design process is a problem-solving technique that proceeds in seven steps:[3]

1. *Acceptance.* In the first stage, you recognize that there is a problem that you want to solve. You state your initial objectives for the process, set aside resources for the effort, and get started.

[2] The concept of emergent planning is based upon the ideas of Henry Mintzberg, *Mintzberg on Management*, The Free Press, New York, Chapters 2 and 3, 1989.
[3] The description of phases of the design process is based upon the ideas of Don Koberg and Jim Bagnall, *Universal Traveler*, revised, William Kaufmann, Inc., Los Altos, California, 1981.

2. *Analysis.* In this step, you begin to put limits on the problem. That involves fact finding, research, and gathering information so you can clarify what you already know and find out what you need to learn. Once you have assembled the data, you look for patterns and relationships; you try to understand each aspect of the problem and how it relates to the whole.

3. *Definition.* Having analyzed the elements, you now define the specific nature of the problem you will solve. You develop and clarify design goals. You assemble all the information and construct an overview of the problem. You define design objectives and specifications and determine the criteria that will be used to evaluate the eventual solution.

4. *Ideation.* In this stage you generate alternatives for attaining the essential goals. You develop possible solutions that meet the criteria you defined in the preceding stage.

5. *Selection.* This is the point at which you have to choose among the options that meet your criteria. You compare solutions with goals and determine the best way to proceed. Here is where you pick your priorities.

6. *Implementation.* At this stage, you move from planning to acting. You detail exactly how to carry out the preferred alternative and you do it.

7. *Evaluation.* This is the final step in the continuing process. You review results, suggest modifications, and begin the cycle anew. Effective evaluation focuses on two aspects: how well you carried out the plan and how appropriate the goals and specifications were in the first place.

Figure 2.1 summarizes the steps in the design process. Though these phases are described in sequence, the design process is not linear. You don't have to proceed through all the stages to modify something that has gone before. If your experience at any point in the process suggests the need to revise earlier decisions, you should go ahead and make the change.

Strategic planning consists of seven steps, each of which is comparable to a step in the design process:[4]

1. *The plan to plan.* The first step in strategic planning is to determine how you will proceed to do the planning.

[4]A more extensive discussion of the steps in strategic planning can be found in George A. Steiner, *Strategic Planning*, The Free Press, New York, 1979.

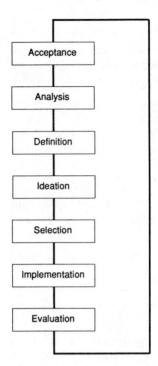

Figure 2.1. Steps in the design process.

2. *Mission.* Design practices are mission-driven organizations. Your mission defines the basic orientation of the practice. It shapes everything the practice is and does. The mission states the basic design objectives for the practice.

3. *Situational analysis.* How successful a practice will be in achieving its mission depends on both internal and external factors. The factors are examined in the situational analysis. The internal capabilities of the practice consist of the financial and technological resources available to it, the talents and abilities of the staff, and the norms, values, and other aspects of the organization's culture. Factors in the external environment include general business and economic conditions in which the practice operates, the specific market climate, the needs of clients, and the nature of the competition. This step is comparable to the analysis stage in the design process.

Central to the situational analysis is the determination of strengths, weaknesses, opportunities, and threats. Strengths and weaknesses are what the practice does well and not so well; they are attributes of your practice over which you have control. Opportunities and threats are trends or forces outside the practice that might affect your ability to progress toward your goals. Though you cannot influence external events, you do control your response to them and the meanings you assign to them.

4. *Goals.*   The next step in strategic planning is to formulate goals. Goals are statements of what the practice wants to achieve in pursuit of its mission. They describe conditions that the practice will meet in the next 3 to 5 years. The formulation of goals is equivalent to the definition stage of the design process.

5. *Strategies.*   Strategies describe how you will achieve your goals. In this step, you determine your alternatives for attaining your goals and decide upon a general approach. This stage combines the ideation and selection steps in the design process.

6. *Operational plans.*   At this stage, you prepare an operational plan for the next year. This plan outlines in detail your objectives and the steps you will take to accomplish them. The operational plan is your blueprint for action for the year. It corresponds to the implementation phase in the design process.

7. *Evaluation.*   The final step in strategic planning is evaluation. You look at your actual performance for the year compared with your objectives. You try to figure out the reasons for any differences that may have occurred. That will give you valuable information about what changes to make in order to improve future performance. Once you complete your evaluation, you are ready to begin a new planning cycle.

The steps in the strategic planning process are shown in Figure 2.2. Effective planning takes time and requires intense, focused thought. The amount and complexity of planning should be appropriate to the practice. You need to determine the level of effort that provides the benefits of planning without being an undue burden on you or your staff.

Appendix A contains several worksheets that will assist you in the planning effort. Larger and more complex firms requiring thorough plans can prepare a comprehensive plan that includes the elements described in the next section. Smaller practices with simpler needs can use either the accelerated planning method or the prospective hindsight method discussed in Appendix B.

Developing the Strategic Plan

Plan to Plan

The first step in strategic planning is to determine how you will go about the process. The plan to plan is the blueprint for the planning

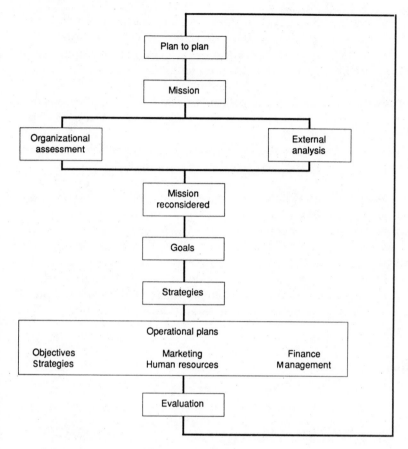

Figure 2.2. The strategic planning process.

effort. It describes who will be involved in developing the plan, what each will do, how long he or she has to do it, and how much detail the plan will provide.

A plan does not have to be long or complex to be useful. A concise plan that guides daily activity in the practice is far more valuable than a comprehensive study that everyone ignores. A few well-chosen goals and objectives can galvanize the organization into focusing on what is really important, whereas too much detail may dissipate effort.

Who should participate in planning depends on whether you want decisions to come from the top down or from the bottom up. In the top down approach, the principals determine the plan and sell it to staff. In contrast, the bottom up approach involves as many people as possible in the process to gain the benefit of their experiences and gain their commitments. People who participate in the process have a greater commitment to carry out the plan than those who are not involved. That is a good reason to make the process more rather than less inclusive.

People's participation should reflect the level of their decision-making responsibility. Principals and others who set policy should be involved in determining mission, goals, and strategy. Staff who have management responsibility for carrying out policies should help develop objectives and operational plans for those areas. That is because those who perform a function usually have the best knowledge and information about those functions. For example, the marketing director should participate in setting marketing goals and preparing marketing plans.

When more than one person is involved in planning, you need to determine how decisions will be made. Issues can be decided by consensus, by vote, or by one person's direction. You can use different procedures for different issues. If people other than principals are involved, you need to determine their role in making decisions. Will they help decide, or will they just make recommendations for your consideration? It is important to let participants know how decisions will be made at the beginning of the process so that everyone knows the rules. (See Chapter 7 for a fuller discussion of group process and decision making.)

Mission Statement

The mission of a design practice governs all the practice's actions. The mission drives the business activities of the practice, which in turn provide the resources necessary to accomplish the mission.

The mission statement is the keystone of a strategic plan; in its broadest sense, it describes what the practice is all about, its basic orientation. Your mission positions the practice in the marketplace and determines the services you will offer. The rest of the strategic plan provides the details of how the mission will be implemented.

There are two approaches to determining your mission. The first, using the traditional approach to planning, is to formulate your mission on the basis of a thorough evaluation of your individual goals, the practice, and the external environment. That is a rational approach; it relies on logic and analysis. Because it assumes that thought precedes action, it works well for those who know exactly what they want, who have a clear idea of what they want to achieve before they set out to achieve it.

But many design professionals don't always know exactly what they want to do. They prefer to explore, to experiment, to act first and figure it out later. Emergent planning, the second approach, is more effective for people who work that way. It is an intuitive and organic process in which the mission forms out of experience rather than being formulated through an idea or an ideology. This approach holds that people always act with a purpose but may not know what that purpose is when they act. Looking at their actions after the fact, they may be able to discern a pattern, and out of that pattern can come the mission.

An example of emergent planning is HWA. When the principals started their firm, they wanted to have a general interior design practice with no particular specialty. One of their early projects, a small hotel, received a great deal of attention. As a result, they did several similar projects. Within 5 years, the firm had developed a significant reputation and a substantial client base in the hospitality industry. Though it was never intended, the orientation emerged from the firm's experience.

A mission statement doesn't have to be extensive; two or three paragraphs are adequate. The key to the usefulness of the mission statement—indeed, of the entire plan—is clarity of thinking. Resist the temptation to get too philosophical. The purpose of the statement is to determine your direction. Remember that the statement is an internal document, and not necessarily a public statement, that sets the course for the strategic plan.

Figure 2.3 presents mission statements from two different firms. Ellerbe Becket is a national architectural-engineering firm with 6 offices and over 600 employees. Hall Hurley Deutsch is a 20-person architectural practice in central California.

Figure 2.3. Examples of mission statements.

Ellerbe Becket

To achieve an architecture of extraordinary quality, an architecture that reflects in its totality the dedication, energy, talent, and initiative of a truly extraordinary organization;

To consistently achieve excellent results through the inspired application of resources form a national network bound together by shared values that are based on a tradition of integrity and professional dedication, and to continuously build on a life-enriching outlook for the future;

To simply be the best that we can possibly be;

In so doing, to provide excellent service to our clients, significant and enduring contributions to our culture and environment, the opportunity for growth and fulfillment of our entire staff, and to inspire the recognition and respect of our peers.

(Continued)

Figure 2.3. Examples of mission statements. (*Continued*)

Hall Hurley Deutsch

Hall Hurley Deutsch is a mid-sized general practice providing a full range of architecture, interior design, and land-use planning services;

Hall Hurley Deutsch provides these services for substantial projects (with exceptions as noted below) that require high-quality design; Hall Hurley Deutsch also develops its own projects;

Hall Hurley Deutsch operates in the entire state of California, but concentrates its activities in the central portion of the state;

Hall Hurley Deutsch demonstrates the value of its services through client satisfaction with projects, staff pride and satisfaction, profitability, the absence of litigation, the contribution of its projects to the growth of internal capabilities, and the recognition of peers and community.

Exclusions:

Hall Hurley Deutsch will not pursue the following project types: hospitals, military, churches, small single-family residences, fast food, and relocatables.

Each of these examples contains all the elements in a mission statement. It describes where the practice does its work, what types of clients it will work with, and what kinds of projects it will do. It also defines how the practice will measure the achievement of its mission (by quality of design, satisfaction of clients, reputation, and so forth). The Hall Hurley Deutsch mission illustrates how one firm defined what it doesn't want to do as well as what it wants to do. Worksheet 1 in Appendix A will help you write a mission statement for your practice.

Situational Analysis

Once you have agreed on your mission, the next step is to assemble information on the internal and external environments of the firm. Then you set out the facts and assumptions on which the rest of the plan will be based. The overview of the firm gives everyone involved a common basis for making decisions.

The examination of the internal environment of the practice is called the *organizational assessment*. The review of the external environment is called the *environmental analysis*. A comprehensive organizational assessment includes the following elements:

Brief History of the Practice. This should include information on when and why the practice started, who the key participants in the practice have been, and what some of the significant projects and who some of the prominent clients have been. It also should identify and describe important turning points or crises the practice experienced and how things turned out.

Statement of Design Philosophy. As a central expression of values for the practice, the design philosophy occupies a pivotal place in the planning process.

Values for the Practice. Every practice has a set of values that governs the way it does business. It is important to spell them out explicitly so they can serve as guidelines as you develop your plan. (See Chapter 3 for a more detailed discussion of the role of values in the practice.)

Description of Current and Past Projects and Clients. A design practice is what it does. If in the future you want to do more of the same, your experience is evidence of your abilities. If you want to change directions, you must build on that experience. This review of projects and clients over the past 5 years (or less, if the practice is new) provides the context for determining future directions.

Financial Trends and Projections. This section presents information on the fees, billings, and profit. For each major category of project it should list the number of projects, the number of clients, the range of fees and the average fee per project, the profit, and the total billings for each of the past 3 to 5 years. You should identify trends and make projections for the next 3 years for each category.

Strengths and Weaknesses. Successful practices build on their strengths and compensate for their weaknesses to create a competitive edge. In this step, you evaluate the resources of your practice to identify strengths and weaknesses. Among the resources available to the firm are money, technology, information, equipment, experience, and the skills and abilities of its employees. You highlight the areas that most affect your practice's ability to exploit opportunities and minimize threats. Since strengths and weaknesses are characteristics of the practice itself, you have control over them. You can act on them directly.

One technique for evaluating resources is to define *critical success factors*. Critical success factors are the elements or attributes of a practice that distinguish success from failure. An easy way to formulate those factors is to examine both your practice and similar, successful practices and ask, "What do they [we] have or do that makes them [us] successful?" An example of one firm's critical success factors is this list compiled by a midsize architectural and interior design practice:

Skilled, motivated staff

Quality design

Ability to respond to change

Strong financial resources

Well-managed organization

Diversified substantial projects

Image of being one of the best

Once you have developed your own list, the next step is to evaluate how well your practice does on each factor (Worksheet 3, Appendix A). Be tough and dispassionate in your assessment. Ask staff other than the principals for their perceptions. Go to people outside the firm for their judgments—they might include past and current clients, consultants, and colleagues.

The situational analysis next examines the external environment in which the practice must function. The environmental analysis consists of the following components:

Environmental Scan. In this step, you survey your operating environment and marketplace to identify trends and developments that may affect your practice. Among the areas to examine are trends in society, demographics, economics, politics, technology, competition, and regulation and legislation (Worksheet 4, Appendix A).

Definition of Markets. In this part of the environmental analysis you examine the nature and growth of firm's markets. Who are your current and prospective clients? How do you now define them? How might you segment current and prospective markets? What are the needs, desires, and attitudes of each segment and how might they change in the next five years? Worksheet 5 will assist you in conducting this analysis.

Competition. Your practice does not exist in a vacuum. Clients and prospects have a variety of choices in meeting their needs for design services. The choices they perceive define your competition. Competition is both direct and indirect. Direct competition comes from design practices that offer similar services. Indirect competition comes from other than design firms that provide services that can be substituted for yours. For example, indirect competition for interior design firms comes from furniture stores or manufacturers that offer design services as a loss leader to get clients to purchase from them.

In analyzing your competition, the first step is to identify who your competitors are. Then you gather information on them. Who are their clients? What services do they provide? What is their fee structure? What are their future plans in regard to clients and services? Worksheet 6 will help you in this effort.

With the information on your competitors and your assessment of the firm's strengths and weaknesses, you can now determine your competitive advantages. A competitive advantage is any difference between you and a competitor that meets three conditions: It is a substantial difference; clients perceive it to be valuable; and it can't be easily eliminated or overcome. The differences may be in knowledge, experience, expertise, services, and so on. Worksheet 7 will help you determine your competitive advantages.

Opportunities and Threats. Drawing on the information from the environmental scan and the analysis of markets and competition, you now can draw up a list of major assumptions on which to base the rest of the plan. The assumptions describe trends in the external environment you think are significant and will continue to be in the future. You then need to figure out how these assumptions will affect your practice; they may be threats, opportunities, or both. (See Worksheets 8 and 9.)

Mission Statement Reconsidered

In the situational analysis, you give careful consideration to internal capabilities and external factors that affect your practice. After completing the analysis, it is appropriate for you to review your mission statement in light of the new information. The review gives you the chance to confirm your mission or change it.

There are reasons why your mission might change. As you and your colleagues grow and gain experience, your goals and interests may evolve. If your practice has expanded, its needs will have evolved. Changes in the marketplace and business environment may cause you to question whether your original mission is still feasible.

Also, there are reasons why your mission should not change. You may find that you are on the right track, that your mission is appropriate and feasible. Or you may conclude that regardless of the circumstances, you still want to continue with your mission. Whatever your decision, it will be informed by your analysis, and not be an arbitrary judgment.

Goals

Goals are statements of what the practice hopes to accomplish within that framework of your mission. If your mission is what you want the practice to be, your goals are what you must do to get there.

Your goals define design objectives for your practice for a 3- to 5-year period. That time frame is distant enough in the future that you can stretch your thinking without being too bound by the present. At the same time, it is not too remote that you totally lose touch with reality.

The situational analysis provides the information for determining goals. You can formulate goals to build on your strengths and compensate for or eliminate your weaknesses. You can also develop goals that will enable you to exploit opportunities and prepare for threats.

In order to have meaning, goals should be stated in such a way that you can measure their accomplishment. For example, one of your goals may be "to achieve design excellence." But exactly what does that mean? To make it useful, you must state objective or subjective criteria for measuring it. Will you know you have achieved this goal by the fact that your projects received awards or were published? Will you measure it by the feeling of satisfaction you and your partners have in the quality of your work? Will you know by the fact that your clients give you repeat work and referrals? Will you know by the attitudes of the users as measured by survey?

Well-written goals have several characteristics. They are stated as outcomes or patterns of behavior rather than as behaviors. They are clear and specific. They are measurable and verifiable. They are realistic and in keeping with the mission and values of the practice. And they are set in a reasonable time frame. Worksheet 10 in Appendix A will assist you in developing your goals.

Resist the temptation to set goals for everything. Having too many goals will dissipate your energy and resources. Limit the number of goals to a manageable number—between four and eight. That will concentrate your effort and greatly enhance the chances that you will achieve them.

Strategies

Strategies describe the approach you will take to achieve your goals. They consist of the intermediate steps you must take to attain those goals. Intermediate steps in the strategy must be both specific and measurable, otherwise it will be difficult to determine whether you have accomplished them.

A technique that is helpful in developing your strategy is the force field analysis. In considering how to accomplish a given goal, there are two kinds of forces: those that assist you in achieving it and those that resist it. Positive forces can come from the practice's strengths, its competitive advantages, and the trends in the external environment you have identified as opportunities. Negative forces can arise from organizational weaknesses, competitive disadvantages, and threats from the environment.

In conducting a force field analysis, you identify the forces and estimate how strong they are. The analysis will clarify the actions needed to reinforce positive forces and neutralize the negative ones. Those actions become your strategy for that goal.

Consider the progression from mission to goal to strategy in the plan for APR Architects. The mission states that APR specializes in the design of educational facilities. The firm has extensive experience with primary and secondary schools, and it would like to expand its work with colleges and universities. One of its 5-year goals is "to obtain at least five college or university projects." The force field analysis identified several positive forces: extensive experience, excellent reputation for design, and experience in specific technologies that may be of particular interest to clients. Some of the negative factors were relatively little specific experience with projects for post-secondary institutions and low visibility and credibility with potential clients.

Using that information, the president of the firm developed specific strategies to overcome the negative forces. To increase its visibility with potential clients, the firm planned a major public relations effort. To increase its credibility, the strategy was to develop several joint ventures with a major international firm that already enjoyed a high reputation for that type of work.

Once you decide on a strategy for a goal, you need to spell out specific actions; the actions are your intermediate goals. When formulating intermediate goals, make them specific and measurable. Ask yourself: "Will someone who is not familiar with the practice be able to tell if we have met this goal?" For example, the goal "to improve newspaper coverage" is neither specific nor measurable; the goal "to have at least one story a month in one of the daily newspapers" is both.

Once you develop strategies for each goal, you must examine how the goals interact. Goals for a firm are interrelated; progress on one will affect, and be affected by, the accomplishment of the others. For example, you may find that one goal must be met before another goal can be addressed. Some goals are more important than others. Since you have limited resources, you cannot do everything at once. Consequently, you must also establish priorities for your goals so you can concentrate your efforts on the critical areas.

Operational Plans

The operational plan describes what you will do in the coming year to meet your goals. That requires several steps:

1. For each of your goals, examine the strategies and intermediate goals to establish objectives that you want to meet during the year.

2. Once you have formulated objectives for the year, determine the strategies to achieve each of them. Like strategies for goals, strategies for annual objectives define the approach you will use to carry out the objectives.

3. Determine action plans for each objective. An action plan outlines the specific steps you will take to meet an objective. It designates who is responsible for each step and establishes a deadline or time frame.

4. Allocate resources. The operational plan indicates how much time and money will be designated for each objective.

Objectives, like intermediate goals, describe actions that are specific and measurable. The difference between the two is the time frame. Objectives refer to things you want to do within a year; intermediate goals take longer.

One of the most common mistakes in writing objectives is to make the objectives too vague. An example of such an error is the objective "to do better public relations." A more specific statement indicates exactly what you will do: "By the end of the year, we will be featured in at least three articles in local or regional newspapers, have one story in a local or regional magazine, and receive at least one award for design."

The operational plan is composed of specialized plans for areas that cut across objectives. The areas include marketing, human resources, finances, and management. The marketing plan identifies marketing objectives for the year and outlines the activities necessary to implement them. Marketing generates the projects, fees, and profit that enable the practice to pursue its other goals. Thus, you need to make sure that your objectives are commensurate with the return you require. At the same time, you shouldn't set the other objectives so high that your marketing activities will not be able to support them.

The human resource plan describes staffing levels required by the rest of the plan. Any changes in the amount of work or the needs for employees become objectives in this plan. For example, a projected increase in the number and size of projects will require a corresponding increase in the number of staff hours. You could do it by increasing overtime, by using temporary staff, or by adding part-time or full-time employees. The human resource plan describes how you intend to meet the need. If you intend to hire new people, the plan will describe the type of people you want.

It is important that you consider your needs for support staff as well as technical staff. You need to determine the kinds of support needed, how you will provide it, and appropriate ratio of support staff to technical staff.

The financial plan outlines the financial resources required to accomplish your objectives. It consists of an annual budget, cash-flow projections, and a profit plan. The annual budget is the keystone of the financial plan. Money is the critical resource that enables you to pursue your objectives. The way you spend money is the most accurate and powerful reflection of actual priorities in your practice. If you want to make sure that people take your plan seriously, allocate funds for the year based on the plan. That will demonstrate that you are putting your money where you say is most important.

Cash-flow projections are necessary to determine whether there will be enough cash on hand to meet expenses. Initially, you may be able to do that for only one or two months in the future. As you gain experience, you can extend the period for which you can make accurate projections to six to nine months or more.

The management plan describes the management resources and activities required to implement the plan. Management resources are the systems, personnel, and policies and procedures that support, coordinate, integrate, monitor, and control the activities of the practice. For example, one of your objectives might be to achieve a specific improvement of project performance in terms of meeting budgets and schedules. As part of your management planning, you would determine your needs for information on the progress of projects. You would also outline ways in which you will meet those needs, who is responsible for the activity, how much money they will have, and a schedule for completing the activity.

Monitoring

You have now reached a critical point in the planning process. Having invested time and energy in developing the plan, the next step is to carry out the plan. A well-constructed plan should play an integral part in guiding your daily operations. To do that requires commitment, organizational discipline, and a system that ensures that you are doing what you set out to do.

Procedures for monitoring and controlling activities keep you on track in meeting your objectives. A monitoring system looks at performance and triggers appropriate responses when tasks are not completed and milestones are not achieved. It provides a feedback mechanism that allows you to take appropriate action. For example, if you find that you are falling behind on meeting an objective, you might modify the plan, put more resources into the effort, or change the objective in light of your experience.

Review your actual performance compared to your plan regularly so your responses to changing situations can be timely. How frequently you monitor an activity depends on its importance and its volatility. Cash flow should be checked weekly. The budget can be reviewed every month as can your marketing plan. If you are in a period of stable growth, you can monitor your human resource and management plans on a quarterly basis.

When monitoring activities, it is important to measure both effort and results. Too often, firms look only at results; but results measure things that have already happened. When you see them, it may be too late to correct any problems. Measures of effort, on the other hand, gauge the amount of energy exerted to accomplish that result. If the effort is appropriate, the more you exert, the greater will be your results. Measuring both effort and results allows you to determine their relationship. You will know how much you have to do to get the desired result.

Evaluation

The final step in the planning process is evaluation; it is also the first step in a new planning cycle. Evaluation allows you to learn from your experience before beginning the process anew. When you evaluate your performance, you look back in order to look forward.

The first task of evaluation is to measure the achievement of your objectives. How many objectives did you accomplish? Did you just meet them or did you exceed them? How well did you do on the ones not accomplished? In addition to this "quantitative" evaluation, you should look at the qualitative aspects of your effort and performance. How well did you do? What did you learn from your effort? What new skills did you acquire? What did you learn about how you approached the effort?

In evaluation, failures are as important as successes, if not more so. There can be many reasons for not accomplishing an objective, and understanding those reasons is an important aspect of learning. One possibility is that your estimate of what you could accomplish was not accurate—it was either too high or too low. Knowing that can help you improve your skills in making projections. The evaluation might reveal that the objective was not met because of an unanticipated weakness. In that case, the evaluation has made you aware of the problem so you can take corrective action.

A third reason for not reaching an objective is that the situation changed because of circumstances beyond your control. By examining the changed circumstances and applying your planning skills, you may be able to devise new strategies to cope with a dynamic environment. By exploring these and other possibilities, evaluation yields valuable insights about the practice's capabilities, your ability to anticipate events in the environment, and your capacity to respond.

Evaluation is commonly used to detect problems with performance. For example, many firms evaluate the way they produce construction documents by monitoring projects for the number of change orders that are due to errors or omissions. They have a general or specific standard for the number of changes that is acceptable. If the standard is exceeded, they take whatever action is necessary to improve performance.

Evaluation can also be used to improve the process. If your practice monitors change orders, you can examine the aggregate data for a year. If the same difficulty has occurred on several projects, it might indicate an underlying problem with the way the documents are produced. For example, the source of the problems might be traced to a particular employee who needs additional training. Your evaluation might reveal a weakness in the way you check the drawings or that the time pressure of tight schedules is causing the technical staff to make mistakes. Whatever the source, evaluation enables you to uncover problems, analyze their causes, and suggest solutions.

Most firms use historical criteria to gauge the success of their practice. These *reactive* factors indicate what has already happened, rather than what is desired to occur. They measure the result of some past action; success by these measures is a reflection of past activities. Examples include rates of repeat business or referrals, design awards, and financial statements.

A few firms, however, do make the connection between the past and the future. They use historical material in a *proactive* way to shape their future. Their business and marketing plans, firm-wide budgets, and design review processes all deal with things that are happening now or that will happen in the future. They enable the practice to shape its destiny.

There is also a distinction between strategic and operational measures. *Strategic* measures—a business plan, client satisfaction, and rates of repeat business—treat the practice as a whole. *Operational* measures, on the other hand, concern only a part of the organization, such as an individual department or project. Examples include a production checklist, project schedules, project budgets, and the number of changes required by errors or omissions.

To get a complete picture of all the elements that contribute to success, a firm should use *both* proactive and reactive measures. Limiting your view to the past will interfere with your taking positive action to shape your future. Looking only at the future will decrease your ability to monitor progress toward current goals and take corrective action when necessary.

Similarly, you must look at both strategic and operational factors. If you focus only on operational issues — day-to-day activities — you will have difficulty integrating efforts of various personnel or departments toward common goals. Similarly, if you concentrate only on strategy, you will be unable to establish objectives for the individual components of the operation.

The two distinctions — proactive/reactive and strategic/operational — are two dimensions of the practice: each reflects a different aspect of the same structure. Combining them provides a new way to integrate seemingly unconnected components of the firm. The relationships are illustrated in a simple model of a four-celled matrix shown in Figure 2.4. Items are assigned to cells in the matrix according to where they fall along each dimension. Use the matrix to select the factors in each area that best indicate the progress of your practice. By choosing from each area of the model, you will get a balanced view of how well you are doing in accomplishing your goals.

Not everyone has the time, resources, or need to conduct the comprehensive planning process described above. Those who want a less extensive approach can choose one of the techniques described in Appendix B.

Regardless of which method you use in planning, it is important that

Figure 2.4. A balanced model for measuring success.

your plan be written. It doesn't have to be long. A two-page plan that is central to day-to-day activities is much more useful than a hundred-page document that gathers dust on the bookshelf. But it needs to be written down.

Something happens when the goals go from the principal's head to the written page. Goals, strategies, and objectives are there for you to see and respond to. It is far easier to refer to written goals than to remember them accurately. A written plan is more real and concrete than anything you can say. If your thinking is clear, your plan will be clear. If your thinking is not clear, the feedback you receive from others will help you to clarify the plan. Finally, an unambiguous plan is a powerful motivator. It gives a clarity of purpose and sense of direction to everyone in the practice.

Recommended Reading

Egan, Gerard, *Change-Agent Skills B: Managing Innovation and Change*, University Associates, San Diego, California, 1988.

Hardaker, Maurice and Bryan K. Ward, "How to Make a Team Work," *Harvard Business Review*, pp. 112–120, November–December 1987.

Hickman, Craig R. and Michael Silva, *The Workbook for Creating Excellence*, New American Library, New York, 1986.

Koberg, Don and Jim Bagnall, *The Universal Traveler*, revised, William Kaufmann, Inc., Los Altos, California, 1981.

Lynch, Dudley and Paul L. Kordis, *Strategy of the Dolphin*, William Morrow, New York, 1988.

Mintzberg, Henry, *Mintzberg on Management*, The Free Press, New York, 1989.

Steiner, George A., *Strategic Planning*, The Free Press, New York, 1979.

3

Transforming Vision into Reality: Leadership and Management

Management is a mystery to many design professionals. Within the profession, ideas of what it means to be an effective manager are often conflicting and contradictory. Some understand management to mean bureaucratic control or to be concerned with business affairs rather than professional issues. Others use the word to suggest concern for the bottom line. Some say effective managers must pay attention to their employees. Still others stress creativity, innovation, and vision.

This confusion is understandable, because the same term refers to many things. To clear up the confusion, this chapter will discuss three meanings of management: management as a set of roles that relate to people, information, and decisions in the practice; management as a set of functions that governs the practice and coordinates the various aspects of it into an integrated whole; and management as a process by which you work through others to accomplish the goals of the practice. Each concept will enable you to be more effective in carrying out the design for your practice. Together, the concepts provide a comprehensive model for managing your practice.

Eleven Roles of a Principal

The first way to look at the principal's work is as a set of activities that relate to the basic nature of management. The activities can be grouped into 11 roles having to do with interpersonal relationships, information, decisions, and expertise.[1] The first set of roles derives directly from the formal authority attached to the position of principal. They involve interpersonal relationships:

1. As principal, you are the *figurehead* for the practice. You are the primary representative of the practice in ceremonial activities. You greet visiting professionals and guests when they want to see "the top person." You attend weddings and birthday parties of key staff members. You entertain important clients. These duties may be routine and seem to lack substance. Still, they are important to other people, and therefore to the practice, and they should not be overlooked.

2. As head of the practice, you are responsible for the work of the practice. You hire staff members and, when necessary, fire them. You motivate and encourage employees, seeing to it that their needs are met through the achievement of the goals of the practice. By carrying out these functions, you act in the *leader* role. This aspect of management is discussed in greater detail later in this chapter. For a further discussion of motivation, see Chapter 5.

3. In addition to activities inside the practice, you spend a significant amount of time with people outside the organization. You have contacts with clients, consultants, contractors, suppliers, peers from practices like your own, community groups, and other design professionals. A major reason why you cultivate these sources is to gather and give information. In making these contacts, you are performing the *liaison* role between the practice and the outside world.

Because of your contacts both inside and outside the firm, you are the nerve center of the practice. From your leader role, you know more — or should know more — about what is happening inside the organization. From your liaison role, you have more information about what is going on outside the firm than any of your staff. Putting that information to use is a crucial part of the principal's job. Three roles describe the informational aspects of the manager's work.

4. In collecting information from both subordinates and outside contacts, the principal acts as *monitor*. You are constantly querying contacts for the latest trends. You are constantly scanning both the internal and

[1] The roles of a principal are based upon Henry Mintzberg, *Mintzberg on Management*, The Free Press, New York, pp. 15–22, 1989.

external environment to find out what is happening. That gives you a unique overview of the practice.

5. Having collected information, the principal must share it with others within the practice. As *disseminator*, you pass information to subordinates who wouldn't ordinarily have access to it. You need to be aware of what information is necessary and helpful.

6. In the role of *spokesperson*, you share some of the information with people outside the practice. You are acting in that capacity when you make a presentation to a municipal agency, a business group, or a professional association. Information is not an end in itself. Its real importance comes as the basic material for making decisions. As the primary decision maker in the practice, the principal acts in four roles.

7. In the *entrepreneur* role, you seek new horizons for your practice in response to a constantly changing environment. You are always looking for new ideas, new projects, new markets or services, new techniques to improve, stretch, and expand the scope and capability of the practice. When you find good ideas, you initiate projects, develop them, and integrate them into the fabric of the firm. As entrepreneur, you initiate change in the organization.

8. As *disturbance handler*, the principal must respond involuntarily to external pressures. No matter how good a manager you are, unexpected events always arise: A client has cash-flow problems and is late in paying; a key staff member quits in the middle of an important phase of a significant project; or a supplier doesn't deliver as promised, sending the project schedule into chaos. Such unanticipated events will happen no matter how good a plan was developed. You have to deal with those situations to keep the practice operating as smoothly as possible.

9. The principal also acts as *resource allocator*. You decide who will get what in the practice. The resources include staff time, money, and equipment. Perhaps the most important of these resources is your time. Access to the principal is crucial for staff who want to complete their assignments.

In allocating resources, the principal, in effect, authorizes major decisions before they are implemented. That gives you the opportunity to review decisions and provides a coordinating function that relates decisions to one another rather than have them made in a fragmentary way.

10. The last of the decisional roles is that of *negotiator*. Negotiations are a way of life for the principal. You work out an acceptable contract with a client or consultant; you arrange a salary and compensation

package with a key recruit; you resolve a conflict over scheduling with two project teams.

11. *Technical expert* is the final role. As a principal, you are constantly called on to be an expert—with clients, with staff, with the outside world. To a large extent, status within the design professions is conferred on the principals who exhibit the greatest technical expertise. That expertise can be in many areas, but the highest status is reserved for those who excel in design.

The Eleven Roles of the Principal

Interpersonal

Figurehead

Leader

Liaison

Informational

Monitor

Disseminator

Spokesperson

Decisional

Entrepreneur

Disturbance handler

Resource allocator

Negotiator

Expert

Technical expert

The eleven roles form an integrated whole; they are not easily separable. One person does not have to do everything, however. The roles can be shared. Nor do the roles have to be performed equally. The significance of each will vary over time according to the situation. The important thing is that someone perform each role within the practice.

The above way to view the work of a manager highlights the central role played by the principal in gathering information. That aspect of your work requires that you find systematic ways to convey information to others. A common complaint among staff is the lack of information sharing with their principal. The time and effort spent in communicating information will be repaid many times over in increased effectiveness, greater efficiency, and better decisions.

The problem of information sharing is even more acute when the management roles are shared. The roles cannot easily be separated unless there is also a way to reintegrate them. If team management is to work, those who are responsible for it must make special efforts to share information fully so that the team can make the right decisions to carry out the goals of the practice.

How well you understand and respond to the pressures of the roles will determine how effective you will be as a manager. The pressures are substantial and they don't allow the luxury of contemplation. The job of a principal is characterized by work overload, frequent interruptions, frequent crises that need responses, and abrupt switches from one thing to another. The principal must be able to deal with that. You can do it by recognizing and giving serious attention to issues that require it and by occasionally pausing to look at the broader picture.

The Four Functions of Management

The second concept of management is as a set of functions that link the various aspects of the practice into a unified whole. Management consists of a complex array of activities that can be grouped into four functions: producer, administrator, entrepreneur, and integrator.[2] Each function has its own focus, and each requires different skills, talents, and temperament for effective performance.

In the *producer function*, the principal is task-oriented. You do the actual work of the office. An architect does such things as planning, designing, preparing construction documents, and supervising construction. An interior designer does space planning, selects materials, draws up specifications, prepares design and construction documents, and supervises installation. In each case, the emphasis is on doing the tasks required to complete a project. The producer function may also involve motivating others on the project to be productive and accomplish the project goals.

When performing this function, the principal also directs the techni-

---

[2] The four functions of management are described by Ichack Adizes, *How to Solve the Mismanagement Crisis*, The Adizes Institute, Santa Monica, California, 1985.

cal work of the practice. You clarify tasks, set objectives, and take action. You define the goals of the practice so that all your people know where they stand and how they must operate. To do well in that function, you need technical knowledge of the field and a strong drive and desire to achieve results.

In carrying out the *administrator* function, the principal sees to it that the work is done as planned. You schedule the work, coordinate various activities within the office, and confirm that things are done. When carrying out this function, the manager serves the goals of the practice but does not determine them; they are set by the other management functions. The administrator function only sees to it that they are implemented. The nature of the administrator function requires an individual who is well organized, detail-oriented, methodical, systematic, and who focuses on follow-up.

As *entrepreneur*, the principal identifies new opportunities and figures out ways to take advantage of them. It is through those activities that the practice adapts to changes in the environment caused by such factors as competition, new technology, and a changing marketplace. In this function, you set your own agenda and initiate action.

Since this function deals with the external environment, the entrepreneur must also act as broker. You are concerned with maintaining the credibility of the practice in the outside world and obtaining the necessary resources to enable the practice to keep up with changes.

To act effectively as an entrepreneur, the principal must have an awareness of the strengths and weaknesses of the organization, be attuned to the marketplace, have the creativity to identify possible courses of action, and be willing to take risks.

The fourth function is the *integrator*. In this capacity, the principal focuses on making the system work from a people perspective. You get the group to compromise; you create a consensus within the organization. An important aspect of this function is to help individuals merge their own goals and risks into group goals and risks. This is done by listening to people and analyzing their contrasting values, assumptions, and expectations. The integrator acts to clarify issues and find threads of agreement.

The integrator is concerned about process, about making or generating decisions so that the people responsible for carrying them out are committed to them. In this function, you are a mentor; you help people in the practice develop their skills and abilities. To be successful as an integrator, you need the capacity to be empathetic. You also need the ability to put aside your ego in order to deal with others on their terms.

Four Functions of Management

Producer

Administrator

Entrepreneur

Integrator

Each of these four functions involves a different perspective on the practice and requires different skills and characteristics. For the producer, the firm is a collection of projects. Time frames are determined by the length of the project, and the top priority is the completion of the project. The producer is also a problem solver.

Administrators are usually conservative. They want stability and predictability, they are oriented to what is, and they focus on the status quo and standardization. The administrator wants to do things right, according to policies and procedures. The administrator sees the firm as a set of structures and systems.

Entrepreneurs thrive on change. They have a need for risk, variation, excitement, and growth. They are idealistically oriented and focused on the future, concerned about what might be. They have a long time perspective, one that will enable their ideas to develop. They see their firms as open systems that are constantly influencing and being influenced by the environment.

Integrators stress human interaction. They are oriented toward interpersonal process. They see their firms as collections of individuals in a team held together by affiliation and belonging. They listen a lot; they take time to seek opinions and integrate them in solutions.

The four functions are both contradictory and complementary. The producer, with an emphasis on the task, is the opposite of the integrator, who stresses interpersonal relationships. The administrator who focuses on details is the opposite of the entrepreneur, who is concerned about the big picture.

Because of the tension between these functions, the principal often sees the one in which he or she is most comfortable as the only one that counts. That principal sees the functions as an either-or situation and excludes the others as unimportant. However, when one function is performed to the exclusion of the others, substantial problems can appear.

In many practices, the single principal functions solely as a producer. He or she doesn't like to coordinate, delegate, or administer the work of the others. When a problem arises, this principal drops everything to deal with the emergency. The practice lurches from crisis to crisis in an unbreakable cycle, while the principal concentrates on the immediate problem without regard to the longer term. Since there is no time for longer-range planning, the practice lacks direction and focus.

Other practices are run by a principal who is an enthusiastic entrepreneur and who sees only the big picture and none of the details. This principal is usually spread too thin, is constantly creating crises and pressures, and gets upset when things aren't done yesterday. Vague in working out the details of an assignment, he or she is impatient with limited accomplishments of the staff. Always shifting direction, the enthusiastic entrepreneur creates stress in the practice because the rest of the organization cannot deal with the top person's constant shifts of focus and interest.

Given the conflicting nature of the four functions, it is unrealistic to expect that any single person will have the combination of talents and temperaments required to carry them out equally well. It is also unrealistic to expect that any one individual will feel equally comfortable in each function. It is necessary, however, to recognize that each function is a necessary and valid aspect of managing the practice.

Each of the four functions must be performed if the practice is to survive and succeed. You have two choices in dealing with this situation. Either you can train yourself to perform effectively in more than one function or you can get others to perform in those in which you are less comfortable.

As a first step, you need to assess and accept your strengths and limitations as a manager. Develop an awareness and knowledge of the roles in which you are least comfortable. Find others whose judgment in these roles you respect, and then listen to what they have to say. Recognize that the other functions have an important place in the practice, even if they are not your preference. If you decide to share the responsibilities, you can hire staff to carry out some of the functions. If you can't afford full-time help, find someone to work part time or as a consultant.

Another way in which you can expand your managerial capacity is to go into a partnership with someone who has complementary skills. Hall Hurley Deutsch, a 25-person general architectural and interior design practice, is an example of that approach. The practice has three principals: a producer, an entrepreneur, and an integrator. The comptroller acts as administrator.

Widom Wein and Cohen has a different approach to the division of functions. The three principals have separated ownership of the practice from its management. They act as a board of directors that sets policy for the practice and hires the management. The director of architecture, who is responsible for technical operations, performs the producer and integrator functions. The executive director, who handles financial and business affairs, performs the administrative function. The principals are free to concentrate on the entrepreneur function and to work on their own projects.

Power

Design is a collaborative activity. At its simplest, the collaboration is between designer and client. More often, it also includes a project team consisting of employees, consultants, client representatives, client consultants, contractors, subcontractors, and users. As principal, you set the goals for your practice. They can be achieved, however, only through the efforts of others.

As the central figure, your primary task is to get these other people to carry out your design for the project and the practice. Management is the process by which you achieve your goals through other people. Power is the energy you use to transform intention into reality.

Power is the potential to influence others to do what you want them to do or to induce compliance with your wishes. Power is a critical resource that exists in several forms. The kinds of power you use and how you use them determine how effective you will be in making the design for your practice a reality.

In general, there are two kinds of power. *Position power* is vested in people by virtue of the positions they hold; *personal power* comes to people from their followers. Every principal of a firm has position power; only some principals have personal power.

Sources of Power

Position

    Legitimate power
    Reward power
    Coercive power

Personal

    Referent power
    Information power
    Expert power

Position power comes from several sources. One source is the legal authority of the principal as owner and operator of the business to do such things as hire and fire employees. Legal authority gives rise to *legitimate power*. Position power derives from the possibility of positive benefits: better assignments, promotions, raises, and recognition. This source is *reward power*. Position power also comes from the fear of a negative consequence: reassignment, demotion, termination, or even physical harm. This source is *coercive power*.

Personal power is vested in individuals by the people they are trying to influence. A principal with personal power has the trust and confidence of both staff and clients. There are three sources for this kind of power. *Referent power* is influence based on one person's identification with another. It develops out of admiration and respect for the principal. *Information power* is based on perceived access to data. To the extent that the principal has, or is perceived to have, information that is not available to others, he or she has information power. *Expert power* is based on special skills, knowledge, talents, or expertise. The principal who is a star designer has great expert power.

You can choose among the kinds of power you want to use and develop. The sources you use and how you use them affect the atmosphere within the practice. Some practices rely primarily on positional power. Typically, they are described as corporate practices. Other practices rely principally on personal power. These are usually the more design-oriented firms that have a strong sense of mission. Still others use a balance of both types of power.

The different functions of management are associated with different types of power. The producer function, with its emphasis on task, relies heavily on expert and informational power. The administrator function depends on legitimate and coercive power. The entrepreneur function uses reward power. The integrator function uses referent power.

Different people respond to different types of power. To the extent that you are aware of how individuals might react, you can choose the appropriate type of power for a given situation. For example, clients are influenced far more by personal power, especially referent and expert power. Professional people respond to expert, legitimate, and informational power; nontechnical employees are influenced by legitimate and reward power.

Power is a resource that may be depleted if it is not used; a principal who does not use his power will lose it. Loss of power will impair his or her effectiveness and ability to accomplish the goals of the practice.

The most potent and effective use of power is to influence people to so change their views, values, and assumptions that they adopt your goals as theirs. This transformational use of power creates a vision and enlists people in the cause to make the dream a reality. A principal who uses power in this way is acting as a leader for the practice.

Another use of power, less potent but nonetheless effective, is to get people to work toward organizational goals without changing their values and assumptions. Individual goals remain distinct from organizational goals, but people see the common interest to be gained by helping you out. This is a transactional use of power in which others achieve their goals by working toward yours. A principal who uses power in this way is acting as a manager.

The poorest and least effective use of power is to induce compliance with organizational goals. This negative use of power by coercion withholds rewards and imposes sanctions if people do not obey. Coercion can compel people to comply with orders, but oniy at a very high cost. A practice based on coercion is a toxic and dysfunctional environment.

Leadership

Leadership makes the difference between success and survival.[3] It is the critical element that enables the practice to transform vision into reality. Its force unlocks the energies, commitment, and abilities of everyone associated with the practice. As principal of your practice, you are expected to provide leadership. If you lead well, you will be effective and the practice will succeed.

Leadership is a set of actions, behaviors, and strategies rather than attributes or characteristics. You can learn to lead. According to Warren Bennis, a noted authority on leadership, "No leader sets out to be a leader. People set out to live their lives, expressing themselves fully. When that expression is of value, they become leaders."[4]

There is no single recipe for leadership, but Bennis has identified several basic ingredients that leaders have in common.[5] The first is a guiding vision, a sense of direction that focuses the energy of both leader and followers. Successful leaders create a focus for action by forging a vision. A clear, compelling vision gives others a reason to invest themselves, an incentive to contribute to the practice. It is a magnet that attracts people's attention.

[3] This section on leadership has drawn from the works of Warren Bennis, *On Becoming a Leader*, Addison-Wesley, Massachusetts, 1989; Warren Bennis and Bert Nanus, *Leaders*, Harper & Row, New York, 1985; James M. Kouzes and Barry Z. Posner, *The Leadership Challenge* Jossey-Bass, San Francisco, California, 1989; and Abraham Zaleznik, *The Management Mystique*, Harper & Row, New York, 1989.

[4] Warren Bennis, *On Becoming a Leader*, Addison-Wesley, Reading, Massachusetts, p. 111, 1989.

[5] The basic ingredients of leadership are described in Warren Bennis, *On Becoming a Leader*, Addison-Wesley, Reading, Massachusetts, pp. 39–41, 1989.

The second is passion, a love for what you are doing and enthusiasm for doing it. A leader is involved in life and in work. When communicated, this passion inspires others. Integrity, the third basic ingredient of leadership, has three elements: self-knowledge, candor, and maturity. Effective leaders know themselves. They recognize their strengths and limitations; they can capitalize on the former and compensate for the latter. Always striving to improve themselves, they have the capacity and discipline to improve their skills. Candor requires honesty in thought and action, devotion to principle, and a fundamental wholeness of being. Maturity is the third aspect of integrity. Maturity is gained through growth, which in turn comes from experience.

The final ingredients of leadership are curiosity and daring. Leaders are constantly searching; they are constantly learning about themselves and the world. They find new ideas everywhere. They are oriented toward action, they are always trying something new in pursuit of their vision. Having the courage of their vision, they are willing to take risks on its behalf.

The vision of a leader is a dramatic statement of potential that people can share and in which they can participate. Vision can be specific or grand. It can be contained in the design for a single building or space, or it can encompass a neighborhood, community, or region. Vision can be expressed in a body of work or in an overarching theory. It also can be expressed as an ideal for a design practice.

The leader must translate vision into concrete images that galvanize followers into action. By making the vision real and by communicating goals and expectations, the leader inspires followers to unleash their energies in productive activity. When followers have a clear idea of goals and expectations, they feel more satisfied with their work, they are more highly committed to their work and to the organization, they are more loyal, and they are more productive on the job.

Leaders make their visions tangible not only by words and images but also by everyday actions. As principal, you are the primary role model for your practice. Your actions communicate your values for the practice. They tell your staff what you stand for. Knowing what you stand for, staff members can align themselves with your values and in doing so become more effective.

The vision of a practice defines what you want to achieve; the values of a practice determine how you will work toward that achievement. Values establish rules for what is important and what is expected within the practice.

People learn your values not only by what you say but, more important, by what you do. People learn your values in several ways. The first is how you spend your time.

Time is your most valuable resource. How you allocate it states more clearly than anything else what is important to you. In a recent study that illustrates the point, the way in which design principals in architectural firms use their time was examined. In signature firms—practices whose style is recognized as the expression of the design principal—design partners spend between 70 and 75 percent of their time designing, no time at all in actually producing drawings, and only 5 to 10 percent of their time in administrative activities. In contrast, design principals in other types of firms spend only 5 to 10 percent designing and the rest drawing, with clients, and in administrative activities.[6]

A second way people learn your values is by the questions you ask when you interact with them. For example, if your conversations with project managers focus mainly on matters of budget and schedule and not on client service, you are sending your people a message about your priorities. Taking their cue from your questions, the project managers will shape their behavior accordingly. They pay attention to what *you* pay attention to.

The third way to communicate values is by your reaction to critical incidents. The way in which you respond to a significant event and the issues you choose to focus on reveal your underlying values and are communicated to your staff. Gaylord Christopher, of Wolff, Lang, Christopher Architects knows that. When his project teams have trouble with contractors, he first wants to know what the problems are and how they might be solved. Only later is he concerned about who is responsible. His response to the situation reinforces the value that the firm is interested in solving problems, not blaming people.

The things you reward comprise another powerful way to communicate values. Here, too, the impact comes not from what you say you will reward, but from the behaviors that you actually reward. For example, there are many practices that give lip service to rewarding outstanding performance but give the same raise to everyone who makes it through the year. Despite the words, the message to the staff is that survival, not performance, gets rewarded.

Organizational values need four attributes to be effective: clarity, consensus, intensity, and reinforcement. Clarity comes when everyone knows what the practice stands for. Many practices codify their values and distribute the document to all employees. Figure 3.1 is an example from the architectural firm of Wolff Lang Christopher. Consensus on values exists when people within the practice understand and agree with the stated values. Values achieve intensity when people within the practice feel strongly that the values are worthwhile. Finally, reinforce-

---

[6]James R. Franklin, *In Search of Design Excellence*, American Institute of Architects, Washington, D.C., p. 39, 1989.

ment comes when the leadership of the firm acts in a way that is congruent with the stated values.

Figure 3.1. An example of practice values.

Unifying Principals

Wolff Lang Christopher Architects

1. *Approach all situations with integrity.* Be honest, open, and fair in all circumstances. Have a social conscience; take direction from the client without compromising integrity.

2. *Be creative.* Challenge the possibilities by examining the obvious. Develop innovation through a detailed understanding of project needs. Be aware there is always the potential to do something meaningful.

3. *Be dedicated.* Be personally committed to and concerned about each project. Honor promises and commitments. Make a meaningful contribution to society.

4. *Maintain open and clear communications.* Communicate openly and clearly. Be available, sensitive and responsive to concerns raised by others, always striving for solutions.

5. *Be positive.* Have a positive attitude. Be supportive of others. Focus on the positive attributes of each project. Gain fulfillment out of doing your best.

6. *Believe in people.* Respect the inherent worth of each individual. Trust in the natural goodness of people. Give others the support and opportunity necessary to do their best.

7. *Work together as a team.* Help one another. Appreciate the contribution of each team member. Invite input from others respecting their opinions and participation. Openly share knowledge and experience.

8. *Strive for excellence.* Aspire to excellence as a goal for all endeavors. Strive to improve the quality of architecture by being creative, knowledgeable, and dedicated.

9. *Be wise.* Apply our knowledge and past experiences to improve each new project. Know your limits, seeking assistance when necessary.

10. *Consistency of process.* Maintain quality and creativity by utilizing a consistent approach and process.

(Continued)

Figure 3.1. An example of practice values. (*Continued*)

---

11. *Allow for individuality and personal growth.* Encourage individuals to utilize their special talents and to pursue personal interests within the framework of the firm.

12. *Be efficient.* Make clear and purposeful decisions. Realize when you reach the point of diminishing returns. Understand the abilities and aspirations of others, matching them with tasks that are both challenging and stimulating.

13. *Manage with goals.* Develop and maintain short and long range goals. Make decisions with foresight. Be flexible and responsive to spontaneous opportunities.

14. *Strive for simplicity.* Develop clear solutions based upon a detailed understanding of project needs. Focus on providing quality architecture. Keep the bureaucracy subservient to the purpose.

Because you set the example for the practice, you need to be clear about your values. The more aware you are of what is important to you—and the practice—the more you can consciously shape and reinforce those values.

In the complex environment of design, one person can't do it all, and the effective leader knows it. No matter how brilliant the leader, a practice is a collective endeavor, and it needs the collective wisdom and energy of all its employees to succeed. A recent study of excellent projects underscores this point. Dana Cuff found that excellent projects are created not by individual genius, but rather by a team of collaborators guided by a well-respected, able leader.[7]

A leader's vision is shared, not imposed. Effective leaders accept and value diversity. They focus energy by showing people who have differing perspectives and interests that they have needs or aspirations in common. Leaders know what their followers feel, and they can identify a common purpose between their followers' needs and aspirations and their own goals. In that way, they create meaning for people. Their vision defines a context in which the actions, behaviors, and feelings of followers have importance and energy.

The ultimate test of leadership is the impact it has on followers. Successful leaders energize followers to accomplish their goals. Rather than push people in a direction they don't want to go, effective leaders attract them and pull them toward a goal they never thought they could attain. Leaders realize their vision by empowering others to act.

[7] Dana Cuff, *Excellent Practice*, report to the National Endowment for the Arts, 1989.

People feel empowered when they think they are doing something that has meaning, something that makes a difference. They feel empowered when they are able to develop and learn on the job, when they gain a sense of competence and mastery. They feel empowered when they see themselves as part of a community of purpose. Finally, people feel empowered when they are enjoying themselves.

The basis of empowerment is trust. You have to trust your employees — their integrity, their commitment, and their competence. The best way to encourage trust is to demonstrate it by your behavior. Be willing to trust others in your practice if you want them to trust you and if you want them to trust each other. Share information with them. Listen to their ideas. Encourage staff members to share information, to listen to each others' ideas, and to exchange resources. Many practices foster that by having regular meetings at which project teams present their work for reaction and comment by the rest of the staff.

Another effective way to empower people is to foster collaboration and cooperation. In a collaboration, people work in conjunction with, and not against, one another. They are committed to a common goal, and thus they have a greater incentive to work together to accomplish that goal. Their efforts reinforce one another and enable them to do more by working together than they could do individually.

Another method of empowerment is creating confidence in others. To do this, several skills are helpful: the ability to accept people as they are, not as you would like them to be; the capacity to approach relationships and problems in terms of the present rather than the past; the ability to treat those close to you with the same courteous attention you extend to strangers and casual acquaintances; the ability to trust others, even if the risk seems great; the ability to do without constant approval and recognition from others.

Leadership is an active process, a process of striking out in new directions, of taking risks. In people's minds, leaders are always associated with change and improvement, with innovation and progress. Leaders are strivers and risk takers, they are always searching for new opportunities to improve the practice.

Leaders are catalysts for change. As the leader of the practice, you provide the drive and energy, but you don't have to be the source of all new ideas. It is just as important for you to recognize good ideas from other sources, to support those new ideas, and to make them happen.

The link between leadership and change means that you need to understand how to get people to move away from the status quo. You also must be able to motivate people to put out the necessary energy and effort to make change happen. (See Chapter 5 for a discussion of motivation and Chapter 9 for a discussion of change.)

To understand what it takes to be an effective principal, it is helpful to know what followers want from their leaders. Results of a number of studies (in fields other than design) indicate that followers expect four things from their leaders.[8] The first expectation is that their leaders have honesty and integrity. They want their leaders to be consistent in their words and actions and clear in their values, ethics, and standards.

The second expectation is that leaders will be competent. Followers need to see that the leader is capable and effective, in both the technical and the interpersonal areas. The third expectation is that leaders are forward-looking. Followers want leaders to have a sense of direction and a concern for the future. The fourth expectation is of inspiration. Followers want leaders to be able to communicate their vision in ways that encourage and stimulate participation.

Skills

Leadership and management are complex processes. To be effective in them, you must have a wide range of talents and abilities most of which are never considered in design school. Among the specific skills an effective manager needs are the following:[9]

1. Peer skills: the ability to establish and maintain a network of contacts with equals.

2. Leadership skills: the ability to deal with subordinates and all that comes with power, authority, and dependence. They include motivating, training, helping, coaching and a variety of interpersonal skills such as communication, empathy, sensitivity, and listening.

3. Conflict resolution skills: the ability to mediate conflicts, to handle disturbances, and to deal with psychological stress.

4. Information processing skills: the ability to build informal networks, to extract and validate information, and to disseminate information effectively.

5. Skills in unstructured decision making: the ability to find problems and solutions when alternatives, information, and objectives are ambiguous.

[8]The studies on expectations of followers are quoted from James M. Kouzes and Barry Z. Posner, *The Leadership Challenge*, Jossey-Bass, San Francisco, California, pp. 15–27, 1989.
[9]The list of skills of a manager is from Henry Mintzberg, *The Nature of Managerial Work*, Harper & Row, New York, pp. 188–193, 1973.

6. Resource allocation skills: the ability to decide among alternative uses of time and other scarce organizational resources.

7. Entrepreneurial skills: the ability to take sensible risks and implement innovations.

8. Skills of introspection: the ability to understand one's own position and one's impact on the organization.

All these skills can be learned, though not always in a classroom. Many can be gained only through experience.

Recommended Reading

Adizes, Ichak, *How to Solve the Mismanagement Crisis*, The Adizes Institute, Santa Monica, Caifornia, 1985.

Bennis, Warren, *On Becoming a Leader*, Addison-Wesley, Reading, Massachusetts, 1989.

Bennis, Warren and Burt Nanus, *Leaders*, Harper & Row, New York, 1985.

Campbell, David, *If I'm in Charge Here Why Is Everybody Laughing?*, 2nd ed., Center for Creative Leadership, Greensboro, North Carolina, 1984.

DePree, Max, *Leadership Is an Art, Michigan State University Press*, East Lansing, Michigan, 1987.

Filley, Alan C., *The Compleat Manager*, Green Briar Press, Middleton, Wisconsin, 1978.

Franklin, James R., *In Search of Design Excellence*, American Institute of Architects, Washington, D.C., 1989.

Hersey, Paul and Kenneth H. Blanchard, *Management of Organizational Behavior*, 5th ed., Prentice Hall, Englewood Cliffs, New Jersey, 1988.

Kotter, John P., "What Leaders Really Do," *Harvard Business Review* pp. 103–111, May–June, 1990.

Kouzes, James M. and Barry Z. Posner, *The Leadership Challenge*, Jossey-Bass, San Francisco, California, 1989.

Lynch, Dudley and Paul L. Kordis, *Strategy of the Dolphin*, William Morrow, New York, 1988.

Mintzberg, Henry, *Mintzberg on Management*, The Free Press, New York, 1989.

Quinn, Robert E., *Beyond Rational Management*, Jossey-Bass, San Francisco, California, 1988.

Tannenbaum, Robert and Warren H. Schmidt, "How to Choose a Leadership Pattern," *Harvard Business Review*, pp. 162–164, 168, 170, 173, 175, 178–180, May–June 1973.

Thomsen, Chuck, *Managing Brainpower Book One: Organizing*, American Institute of Architects, Washington, D.C., 1989.

PART 2

Designing the Practice

4
Designing the Organization

There is no single best way to structure a practice. Instead, the structure should reflect the program for the practice. Like a program for a building or space, the organizational structure defines the functions people have and the relationships between those functions. It determines how many levels of hierarchy there are. It defines where decisions will be made. It determines how specific or general job descriptions will be. It defines how rigid or flexible the organization will be.

For a practice to be productive, its structure must match its situation. To get that match, you must consider several factors; they include the goals and values of the practice, the market environment in which you operate, and the project process you use. The best match occurs when each factor is consistent with the situation and with every other factor. The first part of this chapter will discuss the factors and how they interact with one another.

When design professionals complain about the need to "get organized," they usually think of a specific type of firm. It is one that has a well-defined hierarchy in which people have definite and specific job responsibilities and only one boss and in which procedures are spelled out: the practice is operated by the book. In other words, these professionals think that "organization" means "bureaucracy." But a bureaucracy is anathema to most designers. That is why some practices never get organized.

Bureaucracy is only one of many ways in which a design practice can be organized. In the second part of the chapter, you will learn of four basic types of structures and their strengths and weaknesses. You must become aware of the advantages and disadvantages of each type if you are to make the right choice for your situation. If you do not assess those factors, your practice may be less profitable and less productive than it could be.

When people think of an organization, they are most likely to focus on its formal aspects: strategy, structure, and systems. That is only a partial view of the organization, however. You must view the organization from another perspective if you are to have a full understanding of the complex nature of a practice. This time the focus is on the informal, or softer, aspects of the organization. The third section of this chapter describes those two views of the organization. Knowing how they work together will give you a better understanding of how to design the practice to your specifications.

A practice is dynamic. Like an organism, it grows, develops, and moves through predictable stages. Each stage presents a different set of issues and problems. Knowing that evolution, you can decide whether, when, and how you want to grow. The knowledge will also provide a basis for developing solutions to these issues that make sense in terms of the design for your practice. The final part of the chapter describes the evolution of a practice.

Designing the Practice

Successful practices are structured and organized to match the circumstances in which they operate.[1] Some firms succeed because they can provide designs for a lower price than any other firm; they treat design like a product. The interior design firm that provides a turnkey operation for branch banks and the architectural firm that designs warehouses around a tilt-up building process are examples of such firms.

Other firms prosper because they can provide a wide range of services for a variety of projects; they tailor their services to the needs and styles of a diverse clientele. Clients choose them for their ability to provide experienced handling of projects and to adapt to a client's needs.

The firms in a third category flourish because they provide a singular service. Clients come to them for a special or unique expertise. The interior design firm organized around a master designer with an international reputation is one example of this type. Other examples are architectural firms that specialize in designing highly complex and specialized projects such as high-tech research facilities.

[1] The discussion of the bases for success is drawn from Alan C. Filley, *The Compleat Manager*, Green Briar Press, Middleton, Wisconsin, pp. 154–155, 1978, and Weld Coxe, et al., *Success Strategies for Design Professionals*, McGraw-Hill, New York, p. 11, 1987.

Table 4.1. Three Types of Practices

I	II	III
Organized for efficiency	Organized for service	Organized for innovation
Standard designs	Services tailored to client needs	Innovative solutions to unique problems
Formal, centralized structure	Flexible structure	Flexible, informal structure
Relatively stable environment	Highly complex environment	Highly changeable environment
Strong delivery	Strong service	Strong idea

Practices in the first category have to be efficient in order to succeed (Table 4.1). They operate in a market in which clients look primarily for the least expensive provider and in which there are other practices that provide essentially the same service. They specialize in only a few project types and standardize their project process. Standardization is the key to efficiency. By reducing client involvement and stabilizing the production process, the organization has less need to undergo frequent change.

In the two other types of firms, standardization is either less possible or impossible. Successful practices reflect that reality. Their staffs must be more highly skilled, both technically and in terms of dealing with clients, because the client is far more involved in the project process. Their structures must be more flexible and responsive to change because they must adapt to a variety of project and client types. At the same time, clients of such firms are more interested in quality of service, experience, expertise, and design excellence, so price is less of a factor.

The tension between efficiency and adaptability directly affects the internal organization of the practice. That is best illustrated by the results of a series of experiments in which small groups were given two different kinds of tasks.[2] A task of the first type involved a problem that could be clearly defined and solved by applying a formula. An example is the application of standard designs to specific situations, such as the tilt-up warehouses or repetitive floor plans. To do the task well, the group had to be efficient.

A task of the second type required the group to first define the situation and then develop a unique solution. There were no rules to follow, nor was there a formula to apply. This type of activity is similar to

[2]Quoted from Alan C. Filley, *The Compleat Manager*, Green Briar Press, Middleton, Wisconsin, p. 156, 1978.

the application of a unique design solution to an unusual situation. To do this task well, the group had to be creative.

Groups that were most successful at efficient tasks were organized very differently from those that were successful in being creative. They had a centralized structure with a clearly defined leader. Once they devised the formula, a well-defined structure enabled the group to operate efficiently.

Groups that were most successful at creative tasks did not develop a centralized structure. They didn't distinguish between the leader and members; the members were equal in power and status. Because they had a more flexible arrangement, they were able to generate more creative ideas than other groups with different structures.

The lesson from these studies is that the best way to organize for efficiency is substantially different from the best way to organize for creativity. When you want to be efficient, your organization should be structured, routine, highly defined, and formalized. When you want to be creative, the structure should be flexible, adaptable, and informal. That is why firms that stress design excellence are organized in studios or teams, whereas those that emphasize efficiency are bureaucratic.

Firms organized for creativity will have difficulty in situations requiring efficiency and vice versa. A firm organized to produce excellent design will find it difficult to compete for clients who are looking for the lowest price, because its structure is inherently inefficient. Conversely, a firm organized for efficiency will have difficulty providing innovative solutions to unique problems because its structure inhibits its ability to be creative.

Because of those differences, firms that try to be both creative and efficient will run into problems. If your firm is large enough, you can avoid these problems by establishing separate divisions with different structures. If your mission is design excellence, you should organize the firm to foster creativity. If your mission is to meet the needs of a diverse client base, you should organize to emphasize service. If your mission is to provide design for the lowest price, you should organize to emphasize efficiency.

Your values for the practice also have a strong impact on practice structure. Values establish rules for what is important and what is expected within the practice. They deal with such issues as openness within the practice, professional autonomy, the meaning of design excellence, client service, humane relationships within the office, and innovation. The structure and organization of successful practices are consistent with the organization's values.

Another factor that influences the design of the practice is the market environment. Each market has its own characteristics: client type, client expectations of the project and the service, the level of sophistication of clients, project types, amount of competition, growth, and standards of success. To design an organization that will be most effective in meeting the market's needs, you must know the nature of the market.

Your firm may operate in an industrial market that consists of private businesses needing standard building types, such as warehouses. In this market clients focus primarily or exclusively on price; the quality of design is of little or no concern. If you want to compete successfully in this market, you must organize for efficiency. On the other hand, you may be an interior designer working in a high-end residential market where clients are looking for a unique style. In that market, you need a structure that will provide creative solutions.

Two aspects of the external environment affect the design of the practice: changeability and complexity. The degree of changeability in the environment affects the flexibility of the structure. When things are stable, the organization can predict its needs and standardize its processes. But when things are in flux—when project types change frequently, when each solution is unique, when economic or market conditions are unstable—the practice cannot rely on standardization. The more dynamic the practice's environment, the more organic its structure has to be.

The complexity of the environment influences the degree of decentralization. When a practice is in a simple environment, its structure can be centralized because one person can comprehend the whole situation. As problems become more complex, one person can no longer hold all the information to make decisions. In such a situation you will get better decisions with decentralized decision making because more people are involved.

The final factor that influences structure is the technology of the firm. Technology consists of the knowledge, techniques, and processes a firm uses to do the project. Weld Coxe and his colleagues have identified three different types of technologies: strong-idea, strong service, and strong delivery.[3] These technologies parallel the bases for survival described above. According to Coxe's model, the strong idea firm delivers a singular service and is designed for creativity. The strong delivery firm tailors service to the needs and styles of diverse clients and project types and is designed for flexibility. And the strong-delivery firm is designed for efficiency and delivers design at the lowest possible price.

In an effective practice, each factor must match the situation as well

---

[3] Weld Coxe, et al., *Success Strategies for Design Professionals*, McGraw-Hill, New York, pp. 9–20, 1987.

as be consistent with the other factors. If your mission is design excellence, not only should you be structured for creativity; you should also be in a market where there are clients who want singular solutions and are willing to pay for them. If you want to be a low-cost producer, you must both structure for efficiency and compete for clients who select designers on the basis of price.

A mismatch between organizational design and external circumstances can lead to problems. That is what happened when a national architecture-engineering firm that was organized around the mission of strong service unsuccessfully tried to win a commission for the design of a speculative office building. A contributing factor was the incompatibility of its structure and the situation. Because the firm was organized to encourage creativity, it could not achieve the efficiencies necessary to compete on price. In this case, its structure worked against it.

Organizational Configurations

The design of a practice is based on one of a few fundamental patterns.[4] Four configurations are of particular interest: the entrepreneurial organization, the bureaucracy, the professional organization, and the innovative organization (Table 4.2). Each is well matched to a particular set of circumstances, and each has advantages, disadvantages, and limitations. You need to be aware of those factors when you consider the best way to put your own practice together.

Entrepreneurial Organization

The most common configuration of design firms is the entrepreneurial organization. An entrepreneurial firm is run by a single principal, usually the founder. The organizational structure is simple and unelaborated. There is little or no staff; there is a loose division of labor among the employees; and there is not much management. Because it has little formalized activity and only minimal planning, it may be considered a non-structure.

The principal does everything, and everyone in the practice typically reports to him. Since there are few organizational systems or controls, the principal is the focus of power. He or she alone determines the direction for the practice, usually in an intuitive manner rather than

---

[4] For a more extensive treatment of the concept of organizational configurations and a description of the different types of configurations see Henry Mintzberg, *Mintzberg on Management*, The Free Press, New York, 1989.

Table 4.2. Four Organizational Configurations

Entrepreneurial	Bureaucratic
Simple, unelaborated structure	Formal, machine-like structure
Principal makes all decisions	Highly formal, centralized decision making
No standardization	Highly standardized activities
Organized around principal	Separation of functions
Principal has all power	Power based on position
Responsive to dynamic environment	Works best in stable environment
Single focus limits ability to deal with complexity	Inflexible, difficult to change
Overly dependent on principal	Stifles creativity

Professional	Innovative
Autonomous principals, formal structure	Highly flexible structure
Collective decisions or politics	Decisions based on expertise
Some standardization	No standardization
Autonomous principals	Organized around experts (design or technical)
Power to partners	Power to experts
Can be responsive if no politics	Responsive to change
Problems of coordination	Inefficient
	Demanding internal environment

through any formal or systematic planning procedure. The entrepreneur runs the show. Because it is informal, flexible, and highly centralized through the principal, this structure can deal effectively with change in a dynamic environment. Its informality and looseness also make the entrepreneurial organization responsive to the principal's needs and vision.

Strong attention and dependence on the principal is an important constraint. There is a limit to what one person can know and do, no matter how bright or energetic that person is. If the activities of the firm get too complex, the principal is overwhelmed. If the firm's mission is too broad, the principal won't be able to control it alone. There is also the issue of what happens if the principal can no longer function or is no longer there. One common manifestation of that issue is the problem of transition from the founding principal to a new generation of leadership.

Another challenge for this type of organization is to maintain a balance between the production and the entrepreneurial functions, between operations and strategy. A principal too involved in operations risks losing sight of the bigger picture. A principal preoccupied with grand designs runs the risk that routine operations may be ignored and begin to go awry.

The success of the entrepreneurial firm is highly dependent on the principal's vision. When the vision is charged with potential and is communicated to the organization, it is highly motivating. But when the vision is ambiguous, muddled, or not clearly communicated, the effect is to confuse and frustrate the people in the practice rather than stimulate them.

Many people find the entrepreneurial practice an attractive setting in which to work. It can be stimulating, challenging, and diverse. At some point, however, the most talented employees may feel that this kind of environment restricts their ability to grow. The control of the principal limits their opportunities for wider management and equity participation. Consequently, they leave as soon as they reach that limit. Unless there are provisions for a leadership transition, the practice could face serious difficulties as the principal nears retirement.

Bureaucracies

When most people think of an organizational structure, they envision a bureaucracy. They see a rational structure in which everything is clearly defined and has its place. The organizational chart defines the bureaucracy neatly: It is routine, efficient, reliable, and predictable—a machine. In fact, people often say that a good organization "works like a well-oiled machine." And they don't like it.

If you think about it, the bureaucratic structure is based on the view that organizations *are* like machines; they are instruments created to achieve other ends. (The term "organization" derives from the Greek word *organon*, meaning tool or instrument.) The classical view of organizations, which is still the conventional wisdom, is that organizations should and can be rational systems that operate as efficiently as possible. Implicit in this view is the separation of thinking from doing, that is, of managers from employees. One result was the assembly line on which workers are human machines.

Bureaucratic firms have a departmental (functional) structure with a strong separation of functions. Design is separated from production, which in turn is separated from construction administration. There is also a clear distinction between the operations (design, production, construction administration) and the management of the firm.

Bureaucracies are designed for efficiency. To achieve maximum efficiency, the organization is tightly controlled, and the control rests at the top of the organization. The top manager is the only true generalist, the only one with a broad enough perspective to see all the functions. Everyone else is concerned only with the part of the practice that concerns them.

This mechanistic view of organizations can be very powerful in certain circumstances: when the task is straightforward and routine; when the environment is stable; when the product is repetitive and similar; when the work can be standardized. Under those circumstances, key tasks can be simplified and paraprofessionals can be used. The best examples of the configuration are seen in strong delivery firms.

Bureaucracies have substantial limitations. Since they are designed for stable environments, they are rigid and cannot adapt well to changing circumstances. The standardization that makes them efficient makes it difficult for them to deal with unique projects or with innovation. Many creative people do not like working in this environment because its characteristics run counter to their values. With their focus on efficiency and standardization, bureaucracies seem to have no room for creativity.

Professional Organizations

A third configuration is the professional organization. This type of practice has several principals each of whom functions independently and works closely with clients but autonomously from the other partners. The primary function of the firm is to provide basic supporting services and a pool of employees from which the principals draw to do their projects.

The professional organization has some characteristics of a bureaucracy without being centralized. The technical environment is sufficiently stable that there can be some standardization of the work. But projects are sufficiently complex to require professionals to staff them. That is in contrast with bureaucracies, which employ people who have a lower level of training and qualifications.

Though they operate autonomously, the principals make the basic decisions about the firm collectively. They do so by consulting and negotiating with one another until they reach agreement. The process works best when the principals share common goals and values and are guided by common interest. This common basis allows them to make decisions by consensus. Although it takes time and effort to achieve, consensus enables the firm to be flexible, adaptable, and effective.

When the principals no longer share values and interests, their collegiality breaks down and politics take over. The partners divide into interest groups, each with its own concerns. In this mode, decisions are guided by self-interest, and political factors determine the outcome. When collegiality and cooperation are lacking, it becomes very difficult to innovate and to change the way things are done within the firm. Political decision making results in fragmentation, stalemate, or unsatisfactory compromises that impair the ability of the organization to be effective.

Professional organizations often assign or appoint one principal to manage the firm. The firm then gives the managing principal, rather than the individual principals, the authority to make certain decisions — usually operational decisions that involve day-to-day management. This works only if the other principals are willing to cede authority to the managing principal. If they are unwilling to let the manager manage, the organization will revert to the political mode.

Many of the issues raised by this form of practice derive from the autonomy of the principals. Since the principals operate independently, each might have a way of working and a set of standards or criteria that differ from those of the others. That can lead to a lack of consistency in both the process and the product. It also can lead to frustration on the part of staff members who have to adapt their methods to the principal for whom they are working.

Since the principals hold power individually, the success of the firm depends greatly on their competence and conscientiousness. When a principal is no longer competent or is no longer committed to the practice, the firm suffers. The very decentralization that gives autonomy to the individual makes it difficult for the other principals to enforce standards of performance.

Innovative Organizations

Innovative organizations are designed to create singular solutions. Their structures are highly organic and extremely flexible; they have few if any aspects of routine or formality. Since innovation means breaking away from established patterns, innovative organizations don't rely on any form of standardization for coordination. Frank Gehry's office rejected the notion of establishing a library of details. The reasoning was that such a library would prevent the staff from thinking creatively about the best solutions.

The prototypical innovative design practice is the signature firm, which is organized around the design principal and has a highly fluid, nonhierarchical structure. The principal of one such firm summed up the firm's characteristics this way: "Our firm is flexible, open-ended, responsive to the nature of the jobs and even ad hoc." (Innovative organizations are often called *adhocracies*.) Work is handled by teams that focus on individual projects. Often the team lasts for only as long as the project.

Power is concentrated in those who have knowledge, and it flows to those who have expertise. Within an adhocracy, management is seldom accomplished by giving orders. In signature firms, for example, the design principal coordinates the work of various teams by constantly giving critiques. These critiques serve as a catalyst for creative design rather than as a blueprint for the team to fill in.

A recent study of excellence in design found that outstanding buildings were designed through the collaboration of strong, talented, demanding individuals led by an equally strong and demanding designer who could bring out the best in everyone.[5] Doing that requires great skill in dealing with people. It also requires the ability to use persuasion, negotiation, reputation, and rapport to fuse individual members into a functioning team.

Because the work is unique, design principals spend much of their time personally monitoring the projects. In signature architectural firms, for example, the principals spend 70 to 75 percent of their time critiquing and sketching over the work of their project teams.

Formal planning doesn't work for innovative organizations. Since they operate in complex and unpredictable environments, innovative organizations can't be described as deliberate, other than to say that they will deal with uniqueness. Adhocracies decide things bit by bit: Strategy is formed by actions rather than intent. Thinking and acting, planning and execution, must merge in these organizations to preserve the organizations' ability to respond creatively.

Like the other configurations, innovative organizations have limitations. Since they are designed to accomplish the unique, innovative organizations are not well suited for ordinary activities, which involve routine, efficiency, and repetition—all of which inhibit creativity. The organizational and financial structure of the practice, as well, as its mis-

---

[5] The study of excellence in design is from Dana Cuff, *Excellent Practice*, report to the National Endowment for the Arts, 1989.

sion and values, constrain the ability of the practice to compete in markets that require ordinary activities.

The internal environment of an innovative organization is very demanding. Because of the fluid structure of an adhocracy, there is much ambiguity within the organization. Though highly creative people don't like structure very much, they don't all have a high tolerance for ambiguity. Working in an innovative organization demands a high expenditure of energy at all times. The two factors combine to take their toll to produce a high incidence of burnout.

As with any model, these are descriptions of ideal types. A practice can have characteristics of more than one type, or it can move from one type to another over time. For example, many practices that begin as entrepreneurial or innovative configurations will transform into professional organizations.

Two Perspectives of Internal Organization

The conventional way to understand the internal organization of a practice is to focus on such formal aspects as structure, strategy, and systems, the elements that integrate the various functions of the firm. This is the rational, or hard, model. As helpful as the description is, it is only a partial view of the complex nature of the organization. Another view, the soft model, is necessary to complete the picture. The soft model focuses on the informal and intuitive aspects of the organization. Combining the two perspectives gives you a comprehensive understanding of the richness and diversity of the internal dynamics of a practice (Table 4.3).[6]

The organization chart represents the conventional perspective. Boxes on the chart denote the positions within the practice; each box has a job description that estabishes the specific work-related tasks associated with the position. The description of the position of project manager, for example, details what a project manager does: prepares and monitors project budgets, project schedules, and so on.

The organization chart defines the structure of the firm; it is a rigid or semirigid framework that prescribes how people within the practice interact and communicate with one another. Structures define the formal boundaries of work units. They determine the hierarchy of formal authority. On the chart of a departmentalized practice, for example, the

---

[6] For a fuller description of hard and soft models see David K. Hurst, "Of Boxes, Bubbles, and Effective Management," *Harvard Business Review*, pp. 78–88, May–June 1984.

Table 4.3. Hard and Soft Models

Hard	Soft
Strategy	Mission
Objectives	Shared values
Policies	Norms
Forecast	Vision
Target	Direction
Tasks	Roles
Static	Fluid
Clarity	Ambiguity
Content	Process
Fact	Perception
Structure	Groups
Formal	Informal
Closed	Open
Obedience	Trust
Independence	Autonomy
Systems	Networks
Written	Oral
Know	Feel
Control	Influence
Decision	Implementation
People	People
Rational	Social
Produce	Create
Think	Imagine
Tell	Inspire
Compensation systems	Rewards
Direct	Indirect
Objective	Subjective
Profit	Fun
Managing	Caring

staff is divided into clearly defined departments such as design, production, marketing, and construction management. Each department has specific responsibilities for and jurisdiction over its part of the total work effort on a project. When that part of the work is complete, it is turned over to the next department.

Work units within the structure are linked to each other through information systems. Information in the hard model consists of data and drawings, project budgets and schedules, manpower projections, financial reports, and analyses of billable hours. Information is used primarily to make decisions and assert control over the project and the organization. It is used in such activities as monitoring the progress of projects to completion, determining work loads and staffing levels, and making financial decisions. Because the information is so specifically job-related, it is typically shared only with those who have a need to know.

A fundamental assumption of the hard model is that people are rational beings, that they are motivated solely by their own welfare. People are managed into being productive in two ways. The first is by the exercise of formal authority; in the hard model, people do things because they are told to do them: Authority is recognized, accepted, and obeyed. The second way is to give them external incentives—primarily monetary rewards such as raises and bonuses—and external perquisites.

The hard model is not wrong; it is just insufficient. The soft model completes the description of the organization; it is based on an intuitive rather than a rational perspective. It focuses on interpersonal processes as opposed to content-based activities. In this view, organizations are arrays of roles instead of collections of tasks. The key is the function the person has within the whole, not the tasks the person performs. The roles tend to be ambiguously defined and fluid in their relationships.

To illustrate the contrast between them, consider the different ways the two models define the position of project manager. The hard model defines a project manager's position as a collection of job-related responsibilities: overseeing project budgets and schedules, supervising project staff, and coordinating the work of consultants. Decisions are based on information from project and labor-hour budgets, timelines, reports on percentage of work completed, and so on.

In the soft model, the project manager performs a set of functions instead of tasks. He or she:

- Acts as the leader of the technical staff and the liaison with the client team
- Keeps eyes and ears open for information from the client group and the rest of the practice so the project team can be kept abreast of events that might affect it

- Acts as spokesperson for the project team
- Negotiates between the needs of the client and the requirements of the technical team
- Monitors the project's finances and schedule
- Negotiates with both the client and the rest of the organization for the resources necessary to make the project a success

In the soft model, the organization is seen as an array of groups and networks. To function effectively, members of the groups must trust each other. That trust enables them to have autonomy to act as professionals. In the soft model, openness fosters trust, which in turn breeds autonomy.

In the hard model, information is distributed through the hierarchy. In the soft model, people share information through networks that cut across levels. The purpose of the networks is to distribute influence around the organization rather than to exercise power. The purpose of information is to share assumptions rather to than interpret facts. When people develop common assumptions, they begin to interpret facts in similar ways; as they participate in the process, they begin to own it. The results are that decisions get made more easily and implementation is more effective.

Because the soft model assumes that people are social beings, it looks to their values, feelings and emotions to understand them. It is based on the belief that people are motivated by the desire to create something rather than just do something. It appeals to the imagination, the need to be inspired, and the need to inspire others to achieve their potential. It says that people don't want to just work, they want to have fun at their work: enjoyment is an integral part of the process.

With indirect, nonmonetary incentives, the soft model motivates people to be productive. Rewards deal with the subjective aspects of organizational life, including achievement, recognition, the work itself, responsibility, advancement, and growth. The system is based on caring and learning. It doesn't penalize people for failure; it encourages learning while recognizing that mistakes are an inevitable part of learning.

The perspectives of each of the models complement one another and work together in fundamental ways. Together, they give you powerful tools for designing an effective practice. You can use the soft model as a guide to developing a high degree of mutual trust within the practice, encouraging people to develop networks across the organization, fostering the development of open communication, creating a compensation system based on intrinsic rewards, and paying attention to values and assumptions as well as facts.

Trust fosters the creation of a shared vision and a sense of common purpose. These, in turn, enable people within the practice to feel they have a common mission. The mission is a broad framework within which action plans that provide clearly defined objectives are formulated. Use the hard model to generate action plans that describe specific tasks which will implement the mission.

An effective manager knows in which context people are operating and which context is most appropriate. When one person operates from the hard model and another from the soft model, it is difficult for them to connect. The first talks about facts; the second thinks about values.

Much of the conflict within a practice can be traced to conflicting contexts. In such cases, the best strategy may be to get people talking from the same context. Have them consider their assumptions before focusing on facts: The interpretations we make of facts depend on our assumptions about the situation. When faced with the same set of facts, people with different assumptions come to very different conclusions. It is far easier to resolve conflicts and get decisions when people have a common point of view than when they don't.

The Evolution of a Design Practice

As a practice grows, it changes. What worked when there were three people doesn't work when there are ten or twenty. A firm that is just starting out faces very different problems than one that has been around for 10 years.

Like a person, a practice goes through a sequence of developmental stages.[7] Each stage has a set of characteristics associated with it. How long it stays in a particular stage depends on how fast it is growing. The faster the firm expands the more rapidly it changes.

Within each stage, the firm is relatively stable; but with growth over time, the issues inherent in that stage become critical. The way the practice customarily operates is not sufficient to deal with the new situation. To cope with the problems, the practice has to change. When the changes are great enough, transition to a new phase is made. After the transition occurs, things settle down for another period of stability and growth until the next transition is triggered.

The situations that trigger the transitions are predictable. They are a

---

[7]This section on evolution of organizations is based upon Ichak Adizes, *Corporate Lifecycles*, Prentice Hall, Englewood Cliffs, New Jersey, 1988; Neil C. Churchill and Virginia L. Lewis, "The Five Stages of Small Business Growth," *Harvard Business Review*, pp. 30–50, May–June 1983; and Henry Mintzberg, *Mintzberg on Management*, The Free Press, New York, Chapters 6 to 14, 1989.

normal result of growth, not a sign of organizational pathology. Knowing what stage you are at will help you anticipate and deal with the situations in a systematic way.

Inception

The first stage of development is inception. When a firm first forms, it is primarily concerned with getting work to do and getting the work done. The issues are straightforward: Get enough clients and projects to be viable, expand the client base beyond those that were with it at the start, and get enough money to keep going. The major strategy — the only strategy — at this stage is staying alive.

The founding principal is usually strong in the areas of design and/or production. You may have good entrepreneurial instincts, but you are probably weak in management. In a new firm, the principal does everything: marketing, design, project management, production, and billing. If there is any staff, they work directly for you.

A new practice is personal and informal. There is little hierarchy, and there are few policies, procedures, or systems. The principal talks with staff frequently and informally. If there are any systems, they are organized around people, not tasks. The firm is a one-person show — your show. As principal, you are the practice. Your design and technical abilities are critical. Delegation is a low priority. You can manage in whatever way you desire, even to the point of being a dictator. Decisions often are nonparticipative. Your style drives and shapes the culture of the practice. You are the only person in the firm who has a total picture of what the practice is and where it is headed.

The only thing that counts in a new enterprise is doing; the production function predominates. The firm is always responding to its environment; thinking and planning are a luxury. Since the firm has little experience and no track record, and there is no time to think, there is no basis for planning even if you were so inclined.

At this stage, the firm is extremely vulnerable. It has only a few clients, and each client is critically important. The loss of any one client could be disastrous. The firm also is exposed to market trends and to its dependence on one person. Because of that vulnerability, problems can quickly become crises. Since it has only minimal management resources, the new firm is usually in a constant state of crisis management.

Survival

After a time, you know you are going to make it, at least in the short run. You have enough work to keep going, and you can deliver the work to your clients. The production function is operating smoothly. Your time horizon broadens. The goal is still survival, but now you look toward the long term. You have three or four employees, and the office has a comfortable, informal feeling.

You are ambitious. You want to do larger, more complex projects. Now the entrepreneurial function becomes important. You want to grow, and you look for whatever opportunities are available. But if you decide to grow, you will have to change the way you have been operating. Your role in the firm will be different. With more people on staff, you will have to spend more time managing and less time doing. Because the projects will be more complex, and there will be more of them, you will have to delegate work to others. One of the people you hire may be a job captain or project manager, someone who will take on some of your management responsibilities. No longer will you be able to be involved in everything.

At this stage, you may have 10 to 12 people. You are still synonymous with the practice. You remain heavily involved in design and production work, but less so than before. The firm is still organized around you; if anything should happen to you, it would be vulnerable. You still make all the decisions, because no one else can make them as well.

Now that the staff is larger, people, planning, and systems are more important than at the first stage. The production function is still primary, but the entrepreneurial function also is important. Planning is probably limited to cash forecasting; other systems are still minimal. Communications are still informal, but they are getting more complicated. Business resources are still critical, but the practice can withstand the loss of any one client without catastrophic consequences.

Success

The next transition occurs when the practice grows from 10 to 12 people to 15 to 20 or more. You have proved your ability in the marketplace. Your projects are attracting attention, and you are getting bigger and better opportunities. The practice continues to expand. As you grow, certain complaints get louder: There is a lack of organization, work just is not getting out, there is poor communication, the new people just don't have the same sense of dedication as the old-timers.

You are caught in a bind. On the one hand, clients who expect personalized service from the principal demand your time on their projects. On the other hand, your staff need you to make decisions and facilitate its work. You find yourself spending even less time doing and more time managing.

Management problems are increasing simply because there are more people to coordinate and supervise, the volume of work has expanded, and the projects have become larger and more complex. You begin to realize that the situation is getting out of control.

As new people are added to staff, communication becomes far more complex. The greater number of people has increased the possible combinations of communication geometrically. The old ways of sharing information are no longer adequate. You need more systematic ways to communicate with your staff, and they will necessarily be more formal and more structured than when the practice was smaller.

The communication problem is compounded because people hired recently do not have the same experience with the practice as the old-timers. They do not share the old-timers' sense of mission and commitment. In the old days, you could use shorthand, and everyone would understand. That is no longer so.

Growth has kept you busy. You still don't have much time for reflection, and you are constantly reacting to the environment. Without time for reflection, you risk losing focus and consistency. What you gain in activity, you may lose in direction.

The lack of structure and systems takes its toll in efficiency and morale. The practice needs structure and organization. It needs consolidation of vision and examination of systems. You need to pay attention to how you do things: the administrative function. You need to stabilize the practice to sustain and continue its growth.

This is one of the trickiest transitions to manage. The skills required to manage a larger practice are significantly different from, and sometimes diametrically opposed to, those needed to get the practice to that point. The practice will need more structure and be a more formal place than when it was smaller. You will need more management skills and abilities and more sophisticated management controls. You will have to spend more time on building an organization rather than on running a practice.

You can acquire this additional management capability in a number of ways. If you have the interest and aptitude, you can get management training through college or university executive development programs or extension courses. If your firm has more than one principal, the partners can appoint one of the principals to be the managing principal. Or you can take on as a new partner someone who has management orientation.

To make the transition work, you have to be able to delegate. Delegation helps you avoid becoming overwhelmed by the sheer volume of work. It also allows you to train the additional leadership and management that is necessary if the organization is to grow. If you insist on making all the decisions yourself, you create a bottleneck in the project and management process, one that can choke the organization's growth.

Practices that try to grow without delegating responsibilities risk falling into the founder's trap. That happens when the practice becomes too dependent on the founder, who continues to run the practice with few or if any systematic processes. His or her decisions are arbitrary and unpredictable. Because the principal doesn't delegate, no new levels of management and leadership are trained and developed. All the best potential leaders will leave because they will see that the firm offers them no chance for the growth they want. The people who remain will lack the drive and ambition to keep the practice at the same level. Not only does the practice suffer but the founder will have a difficult time getting any value out of the firm at retirement.

To avoid the founder's trap and sustain growth, the practice needs the stability that systems and structure provide. To achieve that stability involves a number of changes: greater delegation, increasing emphasis on planning and coordinating work both within project teams and throughout the organization, and the development of administrative systems, project-handling and information systems, and administrative policies.

Inevitably, those changes mean that the organization will become more formal and less personal. Both principals and staff must be prepared to do things differently than they did them in a very different environment. This requires a change in the culture of the firm. (See Chapter 9 for a discussion of organizational change.)

A key challenge in this transition is striking the appropriate balance between efficiency and creativity. There is no one right answer to the question of balance. Your decision must be in accord with the purpose and values of your practice. For example, many practices develop standardized libraries of details for use on their projects. They do so to achieve consistency and economy; the library becomes a record of a firm's experience. Other firms refuse to have such a library; they feel that it enables people to become too lazy. They prefer to take the time to develop something new rather than look at what has already been done.

One way to strike this balance is to structure the process, which is the approach of firms like ISD Interiors. Design principal Mel Hamilton explains that ISD manages the process of the project, not the substance. His firm has developed guidelines that establish criteria for the quality of the final product, the relationships, and the documents. The criteria provide a framework within which the designer has flexibility to be creative.

This is a turbulent time for the practice. The transition produces tension between the forces of administration, which promote order, system, and formality, and the forces of entrepreneurialism, which promote free-wheeling exploration, creation, and informality. You may waver in your determination and ability to go through with the changes.

You may delegate authority only to withdraw it at a whim. You may develop policies and procedures only to have the rest of the organization ignore them. But you must continue to experiment until you find the combination that will allow you to grow while maintaining an appropriate level of control.

Recommended Reading

Adizes, Ichak, *Corporate Lifecycles*, Prentice Hall, Englewood Cliffs, New Jersey, 1988.

Adizes, Ichak, *How to Solve the Mismanagement Crisis*, The Adizes Institute, Santa Monica, California, 1985.

Churchill, Neil C. and Virginia L. Lewis, "The Five Stages of Small Business Growth," *Harvard Business Review*, pp. 30–50, May–June 1983.

Coxe, Weld, Nina F. Hartung, Hugh Hochberg, Brian Lewis, David H. Maister, Robert F. Mattox, and Peter Piven, *Success Strategies for Design Professionals*, McGraw-Hill, New York, 1987.

Cuff, Dana, *Excellent Practice*, report to the National Endowment for the Arts, 1989.

Filley, Alan C., *The Compleat Manager*, Green Briar Press, Middleton, Wisconsin, 1978.

Hurst, David K., "Of Boxes, Bubbles, and Effective Management," *Harvard Business Review*, pp. 78–88, May–June 1984.

Mintzberg, Henry, *Mintzberg on Management*, The Free Press, New York, 1989.

Quinn, Robert E., *Beyond Rational Management*, Jossey-Bass, San Francisco, California, 1988.

Thomsen, Chuck, *Managing Brainpower Book One: Organizing*, American Institute of Architects, Washington, D.C., 1989.

5
Building a Staff

People are the materials of your practice. Their knowledge and abilities are your primary product. Their capabilities determine the kind and quality of work you do. They are critical to the achievement of your vision.

You spend more on people than on any other aspect of your practice. Labor costs can account for at least 50 percent or 60 percent of a firm's budget. With that kind of investment, the stakes are high. The firm's profitability indeed, its very existence — is on the line.

One of your most critical jobs is to assemble a staff and get it working. If you manage your practice well, your staff will be motivated and productive. The firm can realize your goals and be profitable. If you manage your practice poorly, your staff will be unproductive or ineffective and disaster can lurk around the corner.

Badly managed firms make mistakes that can lead to liability exposure, financial penalties, bad publicity, and negative word of mouth. When that happens, it is your responsibility and no one else's, since most personnel problems result from poor hiring and supervision.

Some of the most important decisions you make in the practice are about people: who to hire, what to expect of them, how to get the best results from them. Because a design practice is so dependent on people, time spent on managing people is an investment that can yield substantial dividends.

Hiring

Before you hire someone, first design the job. Think through what you want the new person to do and the qualities you want the new person to have so you can find someone who meets your needs. To paraphrase Yogi Berra, if you don't know what you want in a person, you will end up with someone else.[1]

When you design the job, think about what you want the person to do, the kind of work that is involved. Is it design, drafting, project management, construction administration, secretarial, marketing, or a combination? What functions does each category include? Will the person have any client contact? If so, with what type of clients will he or she be working? Will he or she be working with other staff or consultants?

On what types of projects will the new person be working? Does the position specialize in one project type, or does it deal with a variety? Will the position be assigned to only one project or will it serve several projects simultaneously? Will the projects have quick turnarounds or will they be long-term? What type of project process and practice structure is involved?

Once you have an idea of what the position does, consider the talents that are most important for this position. Does the job require design talent? Technical skills? Management skills? People skills? What mix is most preferable? What are the opportunities and requirements for growth and development in this job? How might the job change with the growth of the practice?

Given those characteristics, what other traits do you want in the person who will fill the job? What experience will prepare someone to do well in the job? What attitudes and values does the person need to do a good job in the position?

Analysis will give you both a description of the job and the profile of the ideal candidate to fill it. But reality is often far from the ideal. If you can't find the ideal person, what are your priorities for background and qualifications? In the current market for staff, what is a realistic combination of background and experience?

When you hire someone, you and the candidate have different interests in the decision. Your primary concern is job performance—whether the candidate can do the job or has the potential to do it. That is a function of the match between the candidate's abilities and the job's requirements. The candidate's primary concern is the prospect of fulfilling personal needs, goals, and ambitions by working for you: The candidate's satisfaction and commitment depend on how well the practice can meet those personal needs. Since performance is a product of both ability and motivation, you must be concerned with both parts of the equation.

[1] For a more extensive discussion of hiring, see Albert Shapero, *Managing Professional People*, The Free Press, New York, 1985.

The consequences of poor recruiting are significant. If you hire someone who isn't qualified for the job, the result will be poor performance. If you select someone whose needs cannot be met by the practice, the result will be low satisfaction and commitment which, in turn, will lead to poor performance and high turnover. Either way, the cost to the practice is high. That is why it pays to spend the time and effort necessary to do a good job in recruiting.

Recruiting and Selecting

Hiring staff is a process similar to the one a client uses to select a design firm. First you figure out your needs; next you find potential candidates by getting out the word; and then you screen the pool of applicants to come up with a short list. People on the short list have the opportunity to make a presentation through an interview. Finally, you make your selection.

Once you figure out what you are looking for, you need to find acceptable candidates. Unless you have someone specific in mind, it is to your advantage to consider as many people as possible. The more choices you have, the more likely you will find the someone who most nearly meets your needs.

There are many ways to recruit: advertisements, contacts at colleges, professional meetings, and referrals. By far the most dependable is word of mouth. When you personally know a candidate or get a referral from someone you know and trust, the information is more reliable than that from any other source.

The primary means for getting initial information on candidates is through their résumés. When you review résumés, though, remember that they are sales tools: They are tailored to give the best possible impression of the candidate. You should treat a résumé in the same way and give it the same importance you would a sales brochure.

Résumés are most helpful in providing information on the candidate's background and experience. The best résumés tell you what kind of work the candidate did in the past as well as what was accomplished in those jobs. As you review the candidates' backgrounds, remember that situations—and people—can change over time. You should look for a balance between experience and a potential for growth.

Candidates fall into three groups: yes, no, and maybe. The yeses are obviously qualified; the noes are obviously unqualified; the maybes may or may not be qualified. Unless you have enough yeses to give you some alternatives, you are better off keeping the maybes under consideration through the next round. It is easier to decide against an active candidate than to find someone new.

Candidates who survive the initial screening make the short list and go to the next step: interviews. Interviews are ubiquitous in the hiring procedure. They give you a chance to look at the candidate's work and determine the level of conceptual and technical skills. They are an opportunity to see how the applicant handles him or herself. They also allow you to assess the candidate's intelligence, level of motivation, people skills, achievements, and needs.

The problem is that there are many pitfalls for the unwary interviewer, traps that make interviews an imperfect tool of selection. One trap is relying too much on first impressions. Most people make up their minds about a candidate very early in the interview, usually within the first 5 minutes. The initial impression is also influenced by the order in which the applicant gives information. If you are not careful, you can make a snap judgment without giving the applicant a full opportunity to demonstrate his or her capabilities.

Most people have a stereotype of what the ideal candidate should be like, and they tend to disregard anyone who doesn't fit that image. Not surprisingly, that image is based on their own attitudes, beliefs, and values. If you are not aware of those tendencies, you can be too limited in your judgments. As a consequence, you may hire only a narrow range of people and lose the strength that can come with diversity.

Another common trap is giving more importance to negative than to positive information. Shrewd candidates know that and they limit the amount of negative information they volunteer. Under those circumstances, it is difficult to get an accurate picture of the candidate's weaknesses as well as strengths.

By being aware of the traps, you can avoid or counteract them and get the most out of an interview. Make sure that you spend enough time to get a good sense of the person beyond the obvious and superficial. Avoid snap judgments. Keep an open mind throughout.

Like so many other things, you get from the interview what you put into it. The most important, and most neglected, part of the interview is the preparation. Do your homework; don't improvise the interview. Consider what information you want from the candidate and prepare a list of specific questions. Use the same set of questions with each candidate. A list of standard questions gives you a basis for comparing the responses of the various candidates.

Save time by reviewing the applicant's résumé before the interview. It will show the candidate that you are a professional who values thorough preparation. It also will demonstrate how you run your practice.

It is easy to forget what goes on in an interview, especially if you are seeing several people in a short time. Take notes so you can remember key points. Make sure you have enough time in the interview to get sufficient information to make a reasoned evaluation.

After the interview, talk to others who have worked with the candidate. But be skeptical. Expect that any reference a candidate gives you will be positive: No one who wants a job will give as a reference someone who will speak poorly of him or her. In addition, most references will leave out negative information either because they want to help the candidate or because they are wary of exposure to litigation.

Despite those cautions, it is still a good idea to check out the candidate. Talk to the reference either in person or on the phone; written letters of referral aren't worth much. Verify the accuracy of the information the candidate gave you. Listen to what the reference says, how it is said, and what isn't said. Listen for pauses, hesitations, for places where the person is searching for just the right language. Ask for specific examples of behavior, ability, or attitudes rather than general statements about competence. Careful questioning and listening will enable you to learn a great deal from a reference.

Now you are ready to evaluate the candidates and make your selection. In your selection, focus on strengths rather than weaknesses. Strengths are far more important unless a candidate's weaknesses would prevent the candidate from doing a good job.

Most people base their selection on a gut feeling, but a gut feeling can be deceptive. You can correct for inherent biases by using a standard procedure to evaluate each candidate. The procedure might assess the candidate's strength in each job requirement such as background, experience, interpersonal skills, and technical ability. You can rate each applicant on a 5-point scale, with 5 for the strongest and 1 for the weakest. The score in each area can be weighted to accord with the relative importance of the area. The sum of the weighted ratings is then the score for the candidate.

This process forces you to consider the candidates' qualifications more objectively than you might otherwise. Compare the objective score to your intuitive assessment of each candidate. If the score and assessment agree, your choice is clear. If they disagree, find why there is a discrepancy. The objective evaluation is no more valid than your intuitive evaluation; it merely offers a different way to look at the candidates, one that corrects for certain biases in the selection process. By coming to an understanding of why one person scored better in one type of evaluation than another, you will be able to make the most appropriate choice of candidate.

Socialization of New Employees

Every practice has its own way of doing things, of thinking about itself, and of thinking about the rest of the world. New employees must learn those things before they can function effectively and be productive. The process of integrating a new person into the organization is called socialization.[2]

At first, new employees spend as much or more time learning how the system works as doing the new job. Not yet knowing the rules of the game, they can be confused and cautious. Until they understand the particular perspective of the practice, they will have difficulty communicating with others and developing trusting relationships. Effective socialization frees up the time and energy the employees spend on learning the system by teaching them what is expected. Whatever you can do to ease this entry will help them become effective and productive more quickly.

New employees are concerned about many things. First they have to find out how to do their particular jobs. Even if there are formal job descriptions, each firm has its own particular way of doing things. How much latitude do they have? What kind of autonomy does the practice, and the boss, encourage or allow? What are the peculiarities of the structure and the system and how do they affect the way employees must work? What, exactly, does the job really entail? These are things that new persons can learn only after they have been on the job for a time.

New persons need to know how to work with others. They have to get to know who and what kind of people the others are. They have to learn the rules of the game of how people work together. Are people competitive or cooperative? Do they share information or hoard it? Does the practice encourage and reinforce team effectiveness or individual performance? Do people care about each other or are they indifferent? Those aspects of the organization are not easily or quickly absorbed.

Newly hired employees are also concerned about their relationships with their boss. What is the boss' style of management, and what is the best way to cope with it? How much independence and autonomy will a new employee have now and how much can he or she expect later? How much will the boss trust him or her, and how closely will the boss monitor the new employee's performance?

[2]See Richard Pascale, "The Paradox of 'Corporate Culture': Reconciling Ourselves to Socialization," *California Management Review*, pp. 26–41, Winter 1985, and John P. Wanous, *Organizational Entry*, Addison-Wesley, Reading, Massachusetts, pp. 167–198, 1980.

The new employee is also testing out what behavior is really re-warded. The things a practice says it values and those it actually rewards may be very different. People who are new to your organization are very sensitive to the true nature of rewards.

Ultimately, the new employee wants to find a place within the practice in which to develop personal identity. The new employee wants the practice to provide a reasonable level of satisfaction of personal needs while having the opportunity to make a unique contribution.

Socialization starts with the selection of new employees. It is important to give applicants an accurate picture of your practice and keep expectations from becoming unrealistic. It is also important to understand the candidates' needs and the ability of the practice to meet them. By aligning the candidates' expectations with the reality of the practice, you can increase the chances that the persons selected will find the situation satisfactory.

By presenting a strong and realistic image of the organization and what it is like to work for it, you are letting candidates decide for themselves whether yours is their kind of practice. If you are clear about the values and climate of the practice, a candidate's initial decision to want to work for you becomes the first step in his or her socialization.

Once the person accepts the job, you should have specific mechanisms for integrating him or her into the practice. One of the simplest ways, used by many firms, small and large, is to pair a new employee with a buddy. The buddy shows the newcomer around, explains policies and procedures, goes through the office manual, and conducts a tour to show where things are and how they work.

Some firms, particularly larger ones, have periodic orientation sessions for new and recent employees. Gensler and Associates holds quarterly meetings at which they relate the history of the firm, describe the range of the firm's work, and discuss past and future directions.

Socialization is not accomplished only by formal policies and controls. As the term implies, it deals in implicit social controls. The stronger the social controls in a practice, the less need there is for formal administrative controls. Successful practices combine both social and formal controls.

Socialization is most effective when there is a comprehensive and consistent focus on key values and norms. These are the things we stand for, it says; these are the values that have overriding importance in this practice. To be valid, these values must be reinforced in everyday activities. When values are operational, they provide the foundation of trust between the individual and the organization. They become shared values that represent the mission of the practice.

As they expanded, Wolff, Lang, and Christopher found that new em-

ployees didn't have the same sense of commitment and shared values as
those who had been with the firm in the early years. As a way of communicating their beliefs, the principals developed a formal statement of
values (Chapter 3). They recognized that it wasn't enough to just state
their principles. According to Gaylord Christopher, they refer to their
values every day to guide their actions. They provide a context for doing things in the practice. So, for example, if a project manager encoun-
ters a problem with a contractor or consultant, management invokes the
value:

> Maintain open and clear communication. Communicate openly and
> clearly. Be available, sensitive and responsive to concerns raised by
> others, always striving for solutions.

Management's first response is to seek a solution instead of assigning
blame or trying to avoid responsibility.

Another way the values are transmitted and reinforced is through
war stories and tribal legends. Stories about important events and people in the organization make up the practice's history and context and
say volumes about its underlying values. These stories teach or reinforce the assumptions about the world that the practice makes. They
can be told formally or informally. Some practices use staff retreats or
conferences as opportunities to share these stories and reinforce values.

Values are transmitted more by experience and exposure than by formal indoctrination and the experiences can be planned. At Gensler and
Associates, it's called learning the "Gensler Way." New people are assigned to a team to observe and learn how things are done. Then they
are given a task. When they have completed it, their work is reviewed
and suggestions made how it could be done the Gensler Way. This way
may be different from other approaches, they are told, but it works. After two or three months, the new people begin to integrate the Gensler
Way into their thinking. That is the way they become part of the practice.

Motivation

Everyone in your practice is motivated. When your staff members are at
work, they are always doing something. It may not be what you want
them to do, but they are engaged in some type of activity. As a principal, you want people to perform to your standards and expectations;
the standards and expectations define what a good job is.

There is no universal force that motivates everyone's behavior. Each
person has a unique constellation of forces that drives, prods, pushes

or impels him or her to act in certain ways. You can't create motivation in others; all you can do is to direct and amplify what they already have. Your challenge is to create conditions within which your staff members will increase their motivation to meet your standards and expectations.

To get people to do what you want, it is helpful first to understand how people are motivated. To illustrate the process, which may occur consciously or unconsciously, consider Sara's situation. Sara knows that you want and expect her to do a good job. Before she does it, she wants the answers to some questions: What will happen if I do a good job? How important to me are the results of doing a good job? What is involved in doing a good job? If I try to do this well, how likely am I to succeed? The answers to these questions are based on her perception of the situation rather than any objective reality. What she feels or believes is what counts.

Factors in Motivation

What are the consequences of doing a good job?

How important to me are those consequences?

What is involved in doing a good job?

If I put out the effort, what are the chances I will succeed?

The cycle of motivation begins with Sara anticipating what might happen if she does a good job. On the positive side, she might get a raise, greater job security, recognition, trust, a promotion, a better assignment, more responsibility, fringe benefits, or increased status both within the practice and within the profession. Among the negative results she might avoid are fatigue, boredom, frustration, anxiety, threat of dismissal, demotion, lesser responsibility, or harsh treatment.

Though all those things are possible, some are more likely than others. Before she acts, Sara tries to figure out which ones are most likely. (Remember that this estimate is based on her perceptions, not on objective reality.) You can influence Sara's estimate. Clarify the connection between performance and rewards so that her perceptions of the consequences are accurate. Make sure that rewards reinforce behavior that you want, not conduct that you don't want. Set up a formal mechanism for giving and getting rewards so that Sara knows that the system is predictable, not arbitrary.

Once Sara has figured out the consequences of her performance, she determines how important they are to her. The value of a reward varies from person to person; it is influenced by personal attitudes, personality, values, and needs. What one person finds motivating, another may not want at all and a third may find indifferent. The value also varies over time. Something that was important last year may not be important now, and that which was of no interest in the past may be highly significant in the future.

Here again you can influence Sara's estimate. First, be clear on the rewards your practice offers to its employees. (Rewards are discussed in greater detail below.) When you recruit for new positions, hire people whose needs match the practice's ability to meet them. Figure out the things your employees want and, to the extent possible, provide them as rewards. Match people to their jobs so that they like what they are doing—the satisfaction of doing a good job becomes a reward in itself. Provide rewards that continue to be valued.

The third thing that influences Sara's motivation is her understanding of exactly what is involved in doing a good job: The clearer she is about how her performance will be judged, the more likely it is that she will do a good job. Too often, people are unclear or confused about what is expected of them. Perhaps Sara has been trying to do her best but what that means was never spelled out. Obviously she has her own standards of performance, but unless her boss is specific, she has no way to know whether her standards are the same as her boss's.

You can improve Sara's estimate by clearly describing the performance you want. The more specific you can be the better. There is a simple way to discover how well your staff understands your expectations. Write a description for each of your staff member's jobs as you would like to see it done. Then ask each person to describe the job as he or she thinks you would like to see it done. Compare the two versions to find out exactly how much and where your and your employee's perceptions don't match.

The final factor Sara considers is her chance for success. She estimates her prospects of actually doing a good job if she makes the effort. Several elements are involved in this calculation. Sara has to feel that she can do what is expected. If she has never done this kind of work before, she is likely to feel less confident than if she has had prior experience in a similar situation. Next, she has to feel that she has or will be given the necessary information, resources, and opportunity to perform. Finally, her assessment is influenced by how much confidence she has in and how good she feels about herself.

There are several ways you can help your staff improve their estimates. In the selection process, you can choose people who have high self-esteem. Show them that outstanding performance is possible. Create an atmosphere within the practice that increases people's self-esteem. Give your employees adequate resources to do their jobs. Be clear and realistic about time limits for achieving goals.

Motivation is the product of each of these four factors; if any one factor is zero, motivation will be zero. If the results and rewards of high performance don't interest her, Sara won't try, no matter how much she feels that she can do it. If she feels that she won't be able to make the grade regardless of what she does, again she won't try hard. If she is unclear or confused about what she has to do, she won't put out much effort. And if Sara feels that even if she does do a good job, she won't get what she wants or what she feels she's entitled to, she just won't bother.

Rewards

Rewards play a critical role in motivation. They are the payoff for high performance. When the link between performance and payoff is clear and the result is valued, rewards are effective in motivating high performance. Since the significance people place on rewards is a personal matter, it is important for you to learn what kinds of rewards are important to your employees. Don't assume that an incentive that motivates you is also significant to others.

Rewards are either extrinsic or intrinsic. Extrinsic rewards come from external sources. They are conferred on the employee by others. The most common extrinsic rewards are monetary; they include salary, fringe benefits, bonuses, and profit sharing.

An important characteristic of a monetary reward is that the worth is of the reward comparative rather than intrinsic. That is, a person values rewards by comparing them with what others are getting and with what money will buy. A salary of $25,000 for a junior designer might be adequate in a small city in the south or midwest but would be low in New York, San Francisco, or Boston. A 10 percent raise would be seen as substantial if everyone else were getting only 3 to 4 percent, but it would be considered a demotion if the average for others were 17 percent. Another characteristic of monetary rewards is that they are independent of the task: They come as a result of doing the job but not from the job itself.

Monetary rewards are most effective when they are clearly tied to outstanding behavior. A bonus based on project profitability is more effective in reinforcing teamwork and efficiency than a fixed raise every 6 or 12 months. So-called merit raises given to each employee each year probably have more negative than positive effects: They merely reward people for surviving, and not for doing a good or outstanding job.

Spontaneous rewards have a greater impact than expected ones. In a medium-size architectural office in California, the principal surprised his most outstanding designer with an expense-paid 2-week vacation to Paris. The staff member was overwhelmed, and the effect on the rest of the staff was electric. They cheered this show of appreciation and were spurred to work even harder.

You don't have to send someone to Paris to have a similar impact. Take an outstanding employee to lunch; give out tickets to the opera, the theater, or the ballgame. Treat high performers to dinner at a first-class restaurant, or give them a day off.

Nonmonetary extrinsic rewards include perks, status symbols, and titles. As with monetary rewards, the value of nonmonetary rewards is independent of the employee's task or responsibility. The employee derives satisfaction from them through the recognition they confer. These kinds of rewards need others to recognize and accept them. If they are not valued by others, they have little effect. That is often the case with such titles as "Associate." If the title doesn't mean anything in practice, it is useless as a motivator.

One of the most potent nonmonetary rewards you can give is recognition for a job well done. Employees really value a thank-you or other words of appreciation or any other attention from the principal. Recognize contributions of outstanding employees both in private and in front of their peers. Celebrate individual and team accomplishments at company gatherings or staff meetings. Create occasions where you can highlight achievements in public. Such actions will motivate individual employees to higher performance and energize the entire staff.

The value of intrinsic rewards is measured internally. People measure rewards against their particular needs and drives. Intrinsic rewards come from the performance of the task itself; they include satisfaction, enjoyment, fulfillment, and pride in a job well done or in an elegant solution. They also come from feeling part of a larger group and having the sense of being involved in a larger mission. In the design professions, intrinsic rewards are more important than extrinsic ones.

If you understand people's needs, you can design situations that enable people to get intrinsic rewards. Among the tools you have for this effort are the types of projects a person does, the nature of the work done, the degree of participation in decision making, the amount of responsibility and authority, and so on. One firm formalizes this process by having project managers ask members at the first meeting of the project team what they want to get from the project. One person might want to get certain types of experience, another to learn new skills. The project manager uses that information when he or she develops specific project assignments.

To be effective in improving performance, there must be a clear link between performance and reward. People repeat what is rewarded, avoid what is punished, and drop or forget what is ignored. When people have clear goals, get regular feedback about the results they have achieved, and receive rewards tied to their achievements, they will improve their performance on the job.

Expectations

One of the most powerful ways to influence an employee's behavior is through your expectations; your expectations establish the level of performance in your practice.[3] See Figure 5.1. That is particularly true of the first assignment of a new employee, especially in an entry-level position, because your expectations set standards of behavior for the duration of the employee's tenure in your practice.

Expectations influence the experienced professionals as well. The way you treat employees is subtly influenced by what you expect of them. When you expect more of them, you treat them better and you get better results. When you have high hopes for them, they sense your expectations and work hard to meet them. Seeing their high performances, you reward them and give them even more challenging work. They interpret your response as reinforcing your high expectations. Consequently, they work even harder to achieve a higher level of performance.

That process also works in reverse. If you feel that Jack doesn't have the potential to be a high performer, you deal with him accordingly. You don't give him choice assignments or the best projects. He tries to meet your expectations, but since they are low, he works to a lower standard of performance. His self-confidence and effectiveness decrease. His low level of performance reinforces your initial image of him as an average worker. Both of you are trapped in a self-fulfilling prophecy.

One hallmark of an effective principal is to create high but realistic expectations of performance, and those expectations spur your employees to fulfill them. Less-effective principals aren't able to create such expectations, and their subordinates suffer as a result. It is extremely im-

[3]A more complete discussion of the role of expectations can be found in J. Sterling Livingston, "Pygmalion in Management," *Harvard Business Review*, pp. 121–130, September–October 1988.

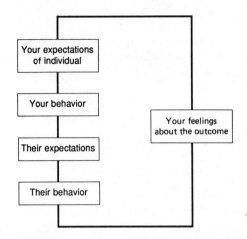

Figure 5.1. How expectations influence behavior.

portant that you monitor your expectations of the people who work for you and guard against the impact of low expectations.

Before they will act on them, employees need to see your expectations as realistic. If they feel that your expectations are too high or are unattainable, they won't even try; they will settle for something less than they are capable of achieving. Nor will your employees be motivated if they feel your standards are too low. They will do just what you ask and not stretch to their potential. Motivation is greatest when people feel that there is at least a 50-50 chance of succeeding.

You can communicate positive expectations by giving employees friendly, pleasant, constructive, and sensitive support and encouragement. Give them help, hints, and suggestions. Provide responsive answers to their questions. Give them regular feedback about how they are doing.

If you don't communicate with your employees, you may still be sending them a message. The absence of feedback or communication is, for most people, an indication of dissatisfaction. Your silence is seen as a sign of low expectations.

Performance Evaluation

Evaluating employee performance is a challenge. The nature of the work makes it extremely difficult to develop objective standards. Since no two people in your office do the same thing and because each individual has a unique style, it is hard to compare one person with another. Even so, you are constantly making informal and intuitive judgments about how well or how poorly your staff is doing.[4]

There are four steps in assessing employee performance:

1. Observe what the person does.

2. Develop standards or criteria that define different levels of performance.

3. Compare the observed behavior with your standards.

4. If there is a difference between the performance and the standard, make a judgment of how important the gap is and what it means.

When you set standards, you are defining what it is to do a good job. There are several dimensions to consider; the first, and most obvious, is performance. Every employee should be expected to do work at a certain level of competence. That much is easy to say and believe. The challenge is to be as precise as possible about what you mean by acceptable and outstanding performance.

At Wolff, Lang, and Christopher, employees are assessed on three dimensions of performance: design ability, technical ability, and quality. McClellan/Cruz/Gaylord, a 75-person architecture and interior design firm, looks at three aspects of performance in its annual employee evaluations:

1. *Quality of design and work.* Quality of design and work encompasses schematic building design, site planning, detailing, composition of construction document package, report formats, letters, presentation ability, coordination of project team, typing, invoicing, blueprinting—all aspects of the services provided to the client.

2. *Project scheduling.* Establishing, maintaining, and producing work on or behind schedule.

3. *Technical proficiency.* Technical expertise in code compliance, plan checking, professional liability, detailing, documentation, and so on.

A second dimension that should be evaluated is the individual's contribution to teamwork. This requires you to describe actions that contribute to teamwork and judge how much the employee's actions en-

---

[4] See Albert Shapero, *Managing Professional People*, The Free Press, New York, 1985, and Edgar H. Schein, *Process Consultation*, 2nd ed., vol. 1, Addison-Wesley, Reading, Massachusetts, Chapter 8, 1988, for a more complete discussion of performance evaluation.

hance or detract from the effectiveness of the project team, studio, or office staff.

McClellan/Cruz/Gaylord looks at several factors including contributions to office morale, participation in and contribution to company activities, teamwork, response to assigned duties, display of initiative, special projects, cost-saving ideas, and participation in management advisory groups.

A third dimension is the employee's relationships with clients. This is important to the extent that the individual has contact with clients. In measuring it, McClellan/Cruz/Gaylord looks at repeat work received, referrals, new client relationships established, clients lost, and comments from clients.

Another performance factor is the employee's contribution to long-term profitability. Firms that use this criterion look at the projects in which the individual is involved and at the level of that involvement. They consider projected profit on the projects. They also examine the amounts and age of accounts receivable. Often, this factor is tied directly to an incentive program. One 15-person architectural firm has developed a profit-sharing program for its employees. If a project shows a profit greater than originally projected, the employees working on it get a share of the excess amount. A large midwestern firm gives bonuses to team members based on their contributions to the project when the project comes in under budget.

A critical part of the assessment process is feedback. Feedback fosters high performance. People do better when they have explicit information on what is expected of them and how well they are doing. Giving feedback allows you to coach your employees, reinforce the habits you hold important, encourage strong performers, and strengthen weak performers. Feedback gives people a basis for comparing their performances, both with those of others in the office and with the standards you have set for your practice.

All employees want to know how well they are doing and where they stand. If you don't tell them explicitly, they will try to figure it out anyway. Without feedback, they will speculate about your assessment, and those speculations will most likely be negative and erroneous.

Here are some guidelines in giving feedback:[5]

1. Make sure that your employees understand and agree to the standards or goals you want them to meet. If you don't have agreement,

---

[5]The guidelines for giving feedback are from Edgar H. Schein, *Process Consultation*, 2nd ed., vol. 1, Addison-Wesley, Reading, Massachusetts, pp. 99–105, 1988.

the feedback you think is constructive may be seen as irrelevant criticism.

2. Emphasize positive behavior or neutral descriptions of behavior instead of negative feedback. The most effective way to reinforce productive behavior is through positive feedback. Negative feedback is less effective because it provokes defensiveness and doesn't provide guidance.

3. Be specific in your examples and guidelines. The more specific you are about both good and bad behavior, the more likely the employee is to understand you correctly.

4. Be clear about why you are giving feedback. If your employees think that you are truly interested in helping, they are more likely to listen and pay attention. If they mistrust your motives, they are more likely to dismiss your comments.

5. Direct your comments to specific behavior and situations, not to the person. That is especially true when you are giving negative feedback. It is more effective to tell employees that you are angry or upset about something in particular than at them in general.

6. Don't withhold negative feedback to avoid a conflict. Because negative feedback often provokes defensiveness, many people avoid it. That just exacerbates the situation. Employees need to know what not to do as well as what to do.

Many aspects of job performance are difficult to measure objectively. That leaves subjective evaluation as the only way to judge certain facets of behavior. The weakness of a subjective judgment is that the judgment can be perceived as being arbitrary and ambiguous. The way to avoid that pitfall is to maintain the credibility of the evaluation process and the people making the evaluations. As long as employees have confidence in the people and the process, evaluation can be effective in improving performance.

Staff Development

Developing the skills and talents of your staff should be one of your top priorities. Expanding the knowledge and abilities of your staff keeps your practice on top of the field and ahead of the competition; it improves your ability to recruit and retain quality people. Young professionals are looking for where they can learn, where they can grow and develop. Providing those opportunities through a staff development program will make your practice more attractive to new recruits and keep your current employees more satisfied, motivated, and productive.[6]

Staff development affects your profitability. The more highly skilled your staff is, the more quickly and efficiently you can complete a project. With appropriate pricing, this enables you to make a greater profit on a project. It also increases your ability to market the firm. Since the professional experience of the staff is your major asset, the more you invest in development, the more marketable your firm becomes.

A primary mechanism of staff development is work assignments. Professional skills are developed through practice, and experience is the key to professional development. Work assignments define the experience that a staff member gets. Consequently, the assignments you give an individual have a tremendous impact on that person's professional development.

In making work assignments, you need to balance the needs of the project with the needs of your staff. Among the factors you should consider are the profitability of the project and the firm, the needs of clients, the need for staff satisfaction, and the needs of the practice for professional development.

Before you make an assignment, you need to know certain things about the project: What tasks are involved? What levels of skill do they require? When is each of the tasks to be done and where? Does the client have any preference for particular staff people? How important is the project to the practice?

You also need information on the development needs of your staff: What types and levels of skill and experience does each of your staff members have? How available are your employees to take on new work? What are their needs for future development? Where are their weaknesses that need to be strengthened or gaps that need to be filled in? What are their preferences for work? How will each staff person fit in with the team leaders?

Many firms evaluate the development needs of their employees as part of their yearly performance review. McClellan/Cruz/Gaylord, for example, annually asks each employee to prepare a career path review that identifies 3-year goals and a plan for achieving them. The supervi-

---

[6] See David H. Maister, *Professional Firm Management*, 4th ed., Maister Associates, Boston, pp. 87–92, 1989.

sor and employee jointly evaluate these goals and determine how the firm can assist the employee in reaching them.

An architectural and engineering firm in southern California has another approach. At the outset of a project, project managers ask team members to develop a personal development agenda for the project. An agenda outines what an individual would like to get from the project. The project manager then uses the agendas as a guide when making specific work assignments.

Work assignments are particularly critical for new employees, since they establish patterns of expectations for the practice. You should treat the first assignments for new employees as the most important event in their tenure at your practice. Make assignments demanding but not unrealistic. Put the employees in situations where they can stretch their talents and do more than they thought possible. Have them work with the best people possible, because the people they work with will influence their perception of the practice.

Other tools of staff development include staff meetings, discussions, and seminars. Each Wednesday, Morris/Deasy/Dilday holds a brown-bag lunch session to discuss some aspect of technical work. The program could be a principal discussing graphics standards for the firm's drawings or a manufacturer's representative talking about product specifications or a new product line. Wolff, Lang, Christopher holds weekly design critiques during which one or two project teams present their latest work and engages the staff in discussion and debate.

Many firms allow their staff to take time off to enroll in classes or to attend seminars, workshops, or conferences. Some firms underwrite all or part of tuition or registration fees. Hall Hurley Deutsch gives each salaried employee an education allowance to be used to pay expenses for classes, seminars, or conferences.

Whether they are formal or informal, most professional development programs focus on improving or expanding technical or design skills and experiences. Few firms pay any attention to interpersonal, management, or leadership skills. Among those that do are Gensler and Associates and ISD Interiors. Each year Gensler sponsors at least one extended program focusing on management or communications skills. ISD Interiors has a series of in-house seminars that include speakers on marketing and management issues.

Conclusion

You compete for staff in the same way you compete for good clients and first-class projects. The supply of talented design professionals is not unlimited, and competition for the best is fierce. Your firm's reputation — as a place to work as well as for the quality of work — determines the quality of employee you will attract.

The most important capital in your practice is human capital. The time and effort you spend in attracting and developing your staff is the most important investment you will make.

Recommended Reading

Filley, Alan C., *The Compleat Manager*, Green Briar Press, Middleton, Wisconsin, 1978.

Livingston, J. Sterling, "Pygmalion in Management," *Harvard Business Review*, pp. 121–130, September–October 1988.

Maister, David H., *Professional Service Firm Management*, 4th ed., Maister Associates, Boston, 1989.

Pascale, Richard, "The Paradox of 'Corporate Culture': Reconciling Ourselves to Socialization," *California Management Review*, pp. 26–41, Winter 1985.

Schein, Edgar H., *Process Consultation*, 2nd ed., vol. 1, Addison-Wesley, Reading, Massachusetts, 1988.

Shapero, Albert, *Managing Professional People*, The Free Press, New York, 1985.

6
Client Relationships

Good client relations fuel successful practices. Satisfied clients are the most important source of new work either through repeat business or by referrals. When clients are pleased, projects go more smoothly, the process is more enjoyable, and morale is high.

The ideal client relationship is one that is both challenging and cooperative. Challenging clients constantly hold you to a high standard of performance. Cooperative clients work with you, not against you. Difficult clients, on the other hand, offer only resistance and criticism, and they generally make the experience of their projects excruciating.

Principals who practice by design manage the client relationship. They know the kind of relationship they want and they establish a psychological contract at the outset. They take conscious steps to shape expectations and build and maintain trust. They confront client resistance directly.

A Primer on Communication

Communication is critical. Arthur Gensler summarizes the centrality of communication to a design practice "The communications process permeates everything we do. We are constantly communicating with the client, verbally as well as visually." Kate Diamond, principal in Siegel, Diamond & Associates in Los Angeles, was asked how she deals with clients who are reluctant to take her advice regarding a design. She said:

> It's simple. I just make sure that they understand what I want and why. If they resist, it usually is because I am not being clear enough in my communication. When I communicate to them clearly, they usually understand and accept my recommendation.

The president of an insurance firm that works closely with design practices asserts that most insurance claims can be traced to poor communication between designer and client.

Communication is a complex process. Think about a time when you met with a client to discuss design options. You began by explaining your approach and showing the alternatives. All the time you were talking, the client was reacting. Her eyes, her body movement, the expression on her face all reflected something about her internal response. She asked questions or commented or argued. You responded with words, gestures, drawings, or color boards. She asked more questions, made a quick sketch, or jotted down some ideas. The process continued until there was some resolution or one of you had to leave.

Communication consists of the messages each of you sends to the other and the messages each of you receives from the other. The messages can be ideas and feelings, verbal or nonverbal, abstract or concrete. They are transmitted in code: words, gestures, drawings, numbers, tone of voice. This sending and receiving goes on continuously for as long as the two of you are together.

You are successful in communicating when the other person has the same meanings for the symbols that you have. Though that sounds simple, it is not always simple to achieve. Situations that seem straightforward can quickly become tangled. That is what the designer for a law firm discovered when she faced a group of attorneys who were irate because their offices were smaller than they had expected. The project manager had explained that the rooms would be 15 feet. by 15 feet. The attorneys interpreted that to mean the total area of each office would be 225 square feet. But the actual area was 210 square feet. To the project manager, 15 feet was the distance from the center of the walls. She knew that the partition took up 6 inches, so the actual area of the office would be smaller. The communication problem resulted because each party understood the same symbol in different ways.

Messages go from sender to receiver by various channels. Speech is sent through sound; drawings communicate by sight; gesture and touch are kinesthetic channels. Most often, people use more than one channel to communicate — sight and sound or movement and touch. Each channel has its own validity, but some channels are perceived as more important than others. In conversation or other oral communication, receivers get only 7 percent of the content from the words spoken, whereas 38 percent comes from the tone of voice, speed of talking, pitch, and so on, and 55 percent from nonverbal cues.

When the message of the words conflicts with that of body language or with the way the words are said, people will ignore the words. That is what is meant by sending mixed messages. Consistent messages in each channel reinforce one another and amplify the impact; contradictory messages cancel each other and cause confusion.

Although nonverbal communication imparts a great deal of information, you have to be careful how you interpret what it means. Certain gestures have accepted meanings: A yawn indicates boredom or fatigue; drumming fingers signal impatience; and a shaking head means no. But body language has no universal vocabulary. Gestures may mean one thing in our culture and something very different to someone from another culture. The only way to really know what nonverbal signals mean is to carefully and sensitively observe the other person's reactions over time.

The environment within which communication occurs can either promote or prevent the process. Any interference that keeps the messages from being understood or accurately interpreted is considered *noise*. Noise can be either physical or psychological.

Phones, loud talking, traffic, and construction all produce sounds that make it difficult to hear and be heard. Visual distractions also create noise that diverts the listener's attention from the message. Because of the possibility of disruptions, it is important to pick or create the proper setting. It would be inappropriate to hold a meeting in a loud restaurant or at a construction site when you want the listener's undivided attention.

Psychological noise, a more subtle and difficult challenge, is caused by the listener's thoughts and feelings. The client may be preoccupied with an event or situation that diverts his or her attention from what you are saying and focuses it on something else. The client may just have had an argument with a business partner or spouse, or won or lost a major contract. For whatever reason, the listener's focus is distracted from the matter at hand, and he or she is unable to concentrate on your points. Another cause of psychological noise is discomfort. If what you are saying causes the listener to be uncomfortable or anxious, he or she may avoid it by tuning out what you are saying.

If you listen carefully and are sensitive to its signs, psychological noise can be reduced in its effects. You can gently point out the listener's distraction by saying, "It seems to me that you are not able to concentrate on this subject right now. Is this a good time to talk, or should we meet at a more appropriate time?" This either will jolt the listener out of his or her preoccupation, or he or she will admit to being distracted and reschedule the meeting. Avoidance is more difficult because it often leads to resistance. Techniques for handling resistance are discussed at the end of this chapter.

Though it is possible to communicate by using all the senses, people usually prefer one mode over the others. Design professionals, for example, are visually oriented, and they prefer the visual mode. They like to see things. In conversations, they focus on visual cues such as what the other person is wearing and what his eyes or hands are doing. They use picture words to express themselves, phrases like "I get the picture" and "I can't focus on that."

Others prefer the auditory mode. They listen with their ears. They pay attention to voice and tone. Auditory communicators use phrases like "That sounds right" and "That rings a bell." Still others use kinesthetics as their primary mode of communication. They concentrate on gesture, movement, touch, and feeling. Typical phrases for a kinesthetic communicator are "That feels right" and "I can't get a handle on that solution."

As you get to know your client, listen for these expressions. Try to determine which way your client is oriented, and then respond accordingly. Match your words to your listener's mode. The client will instinctively understand that you are "speaking the same language," and your message will have a greater impact. Also, the client will trust you that much more.

The ease with which a message can get through is strongly affected by a person's perceptions. Perceptions act as filters; they allow certain information to get in with ease and other information with more difficulty. Some they completely block.

One filter is the listener's self-image. If your client feels knowledgeable about design and the design process, he or she will likely feel confident and deal with design issues directly. If, on the other hand, the client feels ignorant and uneducated, he or she might feel vulnerable and uncomfortable and avoid or resist dealing with the issues. A second filter is the listener's image of you. Again, a client's perception will shape his or her response. If the listener trusts and likes you, he or she will be open to what you say. If the perception is one of untrustworthiness, your suggestions are likely to be greeted with skepticism.

The listener's definition of the situation affects the process. A client who feels that he or she holds the upper hand will probably be confident, even arrogant. One who feels vulnerable will be more cautious and careful, in the hope of minimizing the perceived risk. Expectations also color perceptions. The listener's vision of what he or she wants and how he or she would like people to act influences his or her communication. Vision and wish provide a lens through which the listener perceives the situation.

Those factors, and others, shape and influence the listener's perceptions of the situation, and the perceptions define the listener's reality. Understand the perceptions and you will understand the listener's vision of reality.

When you know the importance of the client's perceptions, you can act to influence them. Understand your own perceptions and expectations and communicate them clearly. Get the listener to clarify his or her assumptions and perceptions so you can determine whether they correspond to yours. If they conflict, you need further discussion. Use the following guidelines to increase the effectiveness of your communications:

1. Be aware of your message. Know what you want to say and how you will say it.

2. Be aware of the listener's response. Be sensitive to the way he or she reacts to you as you are talking. Listen with all your senses to the verbal and nonverbal cues.

3. Be aware of the messages from the receiver. Be alert to both words and body language.

4. Monitor your response to the feedback. Make sure that your verbal and nonverbal messages are consistent.

Listening

Perhaps the most critical communication skill you can develop is listening. You do more listening than anything else: The average person spends 9 percent of his day writing, 16 percent reading, 30 percent talking, and 45 percent listening. Listening skills can be learned. As is true of all habits, before you can change your patterns, you first have to become aware of them.

Listening involves all the senses, not just your ears. Good listeners concentrate not only on the words people use but also on how people say them and what they are saying with their body. Here are some tips to improve your listening:

1. When someone is talking, first focus on what is said and then on what you think is really meant. Are the words, tone of voice, pitch, and body language all saying the same thing? Watch the eyes, the face, and the body, and listen to the voice for clues whether the messages are consistent or contradictory.

2. When you are talking, watch the listener. Is the person really listening to you? Does he or she really understand what you said? Look at the body language. Is the person leaning toward you with interest or fidgeting and yawning? If you feel you are not being understood, check

it out by asking the listener to explain in his or her own words what was heard.

3. Relax and clear your mind. Be receptive to all the messages the other person is sending. As soon as you hear the other person speak, focus your concentration on what is being said. Resist distractions and preoccupation with your thoughts and feelings.

4. Listen to everything the person says. The most common listening trap is to hear only the first few words someone says and then fill in the rest in your mind. When you do that, you block out the rest of the person's message.

5. You can listen much faster than a person can talk. The communication cycle has three phases: listening, analyzing, and speaking. The average person speaks at a rate of about 200 words per minute but listens at a rate of 300 to 500 words a minute. With that time lag, it is easy to short circuit the listening phase and move directly into the analysis phase without hearing what was said. Avoid overlap. Try to listen without analyzing, without interrupting.

6. Don't prejudge the person or the message. Stay open to new information. Avoid emotional overreaction to what the other person is saying—his or her words and ideas—especially if they are different from yours. Hear the speaker out. Let the other person complete his or her thoughts before making a judgment.

7. Take notes of important things to have an accurate reminder of what was said. Most people are only 25 percent effective in listening. Unless you have another way to refresh your memory, you remember only one out of every four things you hear in a day.

8. Listen for intent as well as content. Many people say one thing and mean another. If you are not certain what was said or meant, don't be afraid to ask for clarification. Asking is far better than trying to bluff your way through or misunderstanding what was said.

Managing Expectations

Expectations shape the relationship between designer and client. What you want from a client influences the types of clients and projects you seek, the way you carry out the project, the way you act throughout the project, and the way you want the client to act. The client's expectations are equally important.

Designer A sees herself as an artist. Her conception of the role of designer subordinates the client and user to her intensely personal creative vision. Designer B, on the other hand, sees his role as a problem solver. He views clients and users as collaborators. Designer C considers his proper role to be the instrument of the client. Each of these designers' conception of the appropriate roles of designer and client affects the way he or she deals with clients.

The client's expectations, however, are likely to be different from yours. He or she may be concerned that the project is completed on time, on budget, and with a minimum of hassle, that the building or interior work is as intended, and that he or she gets a good return on the investment. The quality of service may be more important than the quality of work. Issues that are significant to you, such as design excellence, aesthetic impact, and making a design statement, may be less critical to the client.

The key to a successful relationship is getting the expectations to match. The client will be satisfied if your performance meets or exceeds his or her expectations. If you don't meet these expectations, the client could become difficult and the relationship could deteriorate. The results of such a deterioration range from minor irritations to legal action.

It is crucial, therefore, for you to manage the client's expectations so they are consistent with yours, and with your ability to perform. That involves three steps. The first is consciously creating an accurate image in the client's mind of what your practice is and what it can do. The second is understanding the client's expectations. The final step is negotiating any differences to reach a mutually acceptable agreement.

Expectations begin to form during the first contact the client has with you. The way you market your firm, the image you project, and the things you say in preliminary discussions shape the client's perception of who you are, how you operate, and what you can do for him or her.

Some of these expectations are stated in the (hopefully) written contract. They include such items as scope of services, budgets, schedule, and fees. Other expectations concern how you will work together and your respective roles and responsibilities as professional and client. These constitute a psychological contract and are usually unwritten and often unstated. They are, nonetheless, real.

Expectations are like land mines. If you aren't clear about them, they can explode at the worst possible moment and destroy the trust you have worked so hard to develop. That is why a written contract is so important. It is also the reason why you should negotiate a psychological contract in addition to the written one.

The best time to clarify expectations is at the outset of the relationship. An effective technique, according to Randy Morris of Morris/Deasy/Dilday, an architecture and interior design firm, is to have a contracting meeting before the project begins. At the meeting, he reviews the written contract in detail and negotiates the psychological agreement. Having this meeting, Morris says, enables him to reduce problems on a given project by at least 50 percent.

One purpose of the contracting meeting is to review your project process with the client so he or she knows exactly how it will proceed. Clients who are not familiar with the process must be educated about its complexities. You should explain in detail what happens at each stage, who is involved, and what the potential pitfalls are. You should also review each term of the written agreement. (Never assume that someone who signs a contract has necessarily read it and understood it.)

Another purpose of the meeting is to set the client's expectations by describing not only what you would like to do but also what you can realistically deliver. Remember that if you do not perform on your promises, the client will become dissatisfied and withdraw his or her trust. That is why successful negotiators underpromise so that they can overdeliver.

The contracting meeting gives you the opportunity to outline what you need from the client to make the project successful. Some things you might consider are sufficient time to do a good job, access to people and decisions, access to people and information, support from the client, and timely decisions.

You can also explain what the client can expect from you and your office. Among the items to cover are office hours and procedures, the kind of access to you and your staff the client can expect, the times you are and are not available and the best times to reach you, how you handle billing and reimbursements, how your project team works, and how you will work out differences of opinion.

Always clarify your client's expectations. Make sure that you are both on the same wavelength and that your client accurately interprets what you are saying. An effective technique for this is to have the client tell you—in his or her words—how he or she understands what you have said. If his or her interpretation doesn't correspond to your intended meaning, discuss it further until you both come to the same understanding.

Building Trust

Trust is the bonding agent of every successful client relationship.[1] Trust

---

[1]For a more extensive discussion on the nature of trust and and how to build trust see Gerald Weinberg, *The Secrets of Consulting*, Dorset House, New York, 1985.

is the reason you were selected in the first place; it is what keeps the relationship on a positive course and prevents it from going out of control. Put yourself in the client's place. He or she has a problem—the firm is moving to new offices, or he or she is designing a new house or renovating an old one. The client doesn't have the time, the expertise, or the resources to do job without assistance, so he or she comes to an expert—you—to solve the problem.

The client has to rely on you, and in so doing, he or she gives up control. That is a big risk. The person has a lot riding on the project. Self-esteem and the judgment of others hinge on the decisions he or she makes. In the client's eyes, the risk is all his or hers; your risk is small in comparison. When the project is done, you will go on to something else, but the client has to live with it day after day. (This reaction is rarely overt; it is usually subconscious. If you feel it is farfetched, think about how you feel when you have to rely on someone, such as a doctor, a lawyer, or a mechanic, who has expertise that you don't have.)

The client needs to remedy this unbalanced risk. He or she needs some leverage to overcome those feelings of loss of control and vulnerability. The leverage the person uses is trust. Clients will trust you as long as they feel that you will minimize their risks. Whenever a client feels that the risk is too great, he or she will begin to resist and withdraw whatever trust has been given. At the point where trust is withdrawn, he or she becomes a difficult client.

To trust is to have firm reliance on someone's ability and integrity. If clients are to trust you, they must first believe that you are competent, that you can do what you say you can do. They must also believe that you are dependable, that you will deliver on your promises.

In business, trust is not given; it has to be earned. To win a client's trust takes time, but only a moment is necessary to lose it. When someone doesn't trust you, he or she will rarely say so. He or she will just change the way he or she deals with you. That is why you cannot take any client relationship for granted; you must always monitor it. By being sensitive, you can pick up early warning signs of deterioration, flush out and confront the feelings, and get the relationship back on track.

There are several ways to maintain and increase trust. One of the most important is to be reliable. Reliability means consistency and constancy. It means that the client knows what to expect from you. It means that you always do what you say you will do. It means that there are no surprises. It means you don't promise what you can't deliver. When the situation changes from what the client expects, inform him or her as soon as possible in a direct manner.

A second way to reinforce trust is not to use excuses. The client is not interested in why you didn't meet the schedule or why you overspent.

The thing that matters is that the deadline wasn't met or the budget was busted. Excuses are words; only actions count.

You can build trust by listening. Listening shows that you care, that you are concerned, that you are sensitive to your clients' needs and feelings. Listening is also important in dealing with resistance. If you want your clients to trust you, you must first trust your clients. Trust them and their integrity, but be sure they have the facts straight. The saying is, "Trust, but verify." Check your facts. Remember that most people do not consciously mislead you. They may shape reality by simplifying or omitting facts or by smoothing over rough edges, but they don't intentionally lie. They tell the truth as they see it, but their perception of the truth may differ from yours.

Keep in mind that people remember your actions, not your words. If, for example, you provide an extra service to a client without charge, he or she will expect that service—free—in the future. The client remembers only having gotten the service, not that you said "just this one time."

People always remember a promise. That is why it is better not to promise anything than to promise what you can't deliver. If you have no control over an event, as when furniture or equipment will be shipped, don't go out on a limb to guarantee a delivery date. Though it is tempting to try to mollify an anxious client, it can backfire later. According to the president of an insurance agency specializing in the design professions, overpromising and underperformance are a significant cause of legal action against design firms.

A client's trust is based on expectations of what you can—and can't—do. By managing client expectations so that they match your ability to perform, you create the climate for trust as well as satisfaction.

Dealing With Resistance

One of the greatest frustrations you can experience as a designer is to have a client reject your ideas. As a professional, you like to think that you understand the client's problem better than the client does; after all, that's why you were hired. Yet there are times when no matter what you say or do, the client resists your solutions.

Though client resistance can be an aggravating experience, its occurrence can be a positive sign. For the client to offer no resistance, you would always have to be right. In order for you to be right all the time, you would have to be perfect. To most designers, perfection is too high a price to pay for not having to deal with resistance. Resistance also gives you a chance to test your ideas. A client's resistance is an indication that he or she is involved in the process. It is an emotional response to what you are proposing.

Resistance is the indirect expression of underlying feelings. The source might be fear of being dependent on someone else, of losing control, or of feeling vulnerable and at risk. As long as the underlying feeling is unresolved, the resistance will persist.

Dealing with resistance takes special skills.[2] You must be able to sense when resistance is taking place. You must accept resistance as a natural process that can be used in a positive way. You must be able to support the client in identifying the source of the resistance directly. Finally, you must understand that resistance is a natural process, not a personal attack on your abilities.

The first instinct when encountering resistance is to resist in turn. You want to fight harder to get the client to accept your point. But that response is self-defeating. Your resistance can provoke a contest of wills. The client becomes even more determined in his resistance; both of you dig in your heels for a protracted struggle. The result is either an impasse or a power play. You may win the power play—but at risk of losing the relationship. A more productive approach is to work with the client's resistance and get it out in the open. Dealing with resistance is a three step process:

1. Recognize that resistance is taking place.

2. Name the form of resistance in a neutral way.

3. Be quiet and let the client respond.

Resistance can be overt or subtle. Because resistance is a symptom of deeper feelings, your client may not even be consciously aware that he or she is resisting. Consequently, you need to be sensitive to its presence. One of the best indications of client resistance is your response. Be aware of your behavior. When you start getting defensive, impatient, bored, or confused, you should begin to suspect that the client is resisting.

Other signs signal the possibility of resistance. The client may be giving out double messages—the words say one thing but the tone of voice and body language suggest something different. Be aware of nonverbal messages—though the client may not be speaking, the body may be telegraphing a message of resistance. While each individual has his or her own nonverbal vocabulary, certain gestures or postures can generally be

---

[2] The technique for dealing with resistance is described in further detail in Peter Block, *Flawless Consulting*, University Associates, San Diego, California, Chapters 8-9, pp. 113–138, 1981.

interpreted as signs of negative response: physical withdrawal, folding the arms, clenching the jaw, and avoiding eye contact.

Resistance can take many forms:

1. The client keeps asking for more detail. No matter how much you give, he or she always wants more.

2. The client overwhelms you with details. When you ask a simple question, you receive an overlong history. The more information given, the less comprehensible the situation becomes.

3. The client is always too busy to give you his or her undivided attention. Getting decisions is like pulling teeth. Whenever you have a meeting, there are constant interruptions by phone calls or visitors.

4. The client attacks you directly. This is the most blatant form of resistance.

5. The client is constantly asking for clarification. He or she goes over the same point time after time. Asking for clarification is legitimate, but when the same question is asked for the third or fourth time and the client is still confused, that may be a sign of resistance.

6. The client is passive, even impassive. As you make suggestions, there is very little response, if any at all. The client may say that he or she doesn't have much reaction to your ideas. *Never interpret silence as consent.* Silence may mean that the person is avoiding taking a stand, or it could be a way of fighting you. Lack of involvement and enthusiasm may be signaling resistance.

7. Total agreement. If the client offers no negatives at all, be on guard. Every client has at least some ambivalence. When he or she agrees with everything you say, it may be a warning sign that resistance is present.

Once you suspect that resistance is taking place, you must guard against personalizing it. Remember that it is a reflection of fundamental feelings within the person resisting, not a response to you. The natural tendency is to resist the resistance: to withdraw, get angry, or become argumentative. You can avoid that kind of self-defeating response. When you suspect that resistance is taking place, listen more carefully to your own messages to prevent becoming defensive or aggressive.

Once you decide that the client is resisting, your next step is to name the resistance in a neutral way. Avoid blaming the client or characterizing his behavior. Describe the behavior in a way that is not judgmental or accusing and that will open the discussion. One way to do that is to use "I messages": state the effect of the behavior in terms of your reaction to it. By taking that approach, you avoid accusations. The client can respond to your interpretation rather than defend against your assertion. Here are some examples:

- If the person is giving you too much detail, you can say, "I'm getting more detail than I need. Can you describe it in a short statement?"
- If the person is giving you too little detail: "You are giving me very short answers. Could you say more?"
- If the client is constantly changing subjects: "It seems to me that the subject keeps shifting. Could we focus on one area at a time?"
- If the client is totally compliant: "You seem willing to do anything I suggest. I can't tell what you are really feeling."
- If the client just sits there and says nothing: "You are very quiet. I don't know how to read your silence."
- If the client attacks: "You are questioning me a great deal. It seems to me you are angry about something."
- If the client is inattentive or otherwise not involved: "I have the feeling that you have other things on your mind."

Once you have named the resistance, the third step is to be quiet. That is the most difficult part of the process. Your silence will build tension, and tension is the catalyst to get the source of the resistance out into the open. Be patient. Let the client respond to what you have said; let him or her take responsibility for the problem.

Once the true source of resistance is known, the two of you can begin to deal with it. Often, the act of identifying the source will be sufficient to dispel the anxiety and reduce the resistance. The client will find that the problem is greater in anticipation than in reality; when it is finally brought to light, the irrational fear evaporates. This approach will not work, however, if you are more interested in what you want than in what the client wants. Clients are more interested in what they want.

There are ways of preventing resistance. Clients begin resisting when they perceive that they will lose more by following your suggestions than they will gain. Most resistance comes from uncertainty. The more you can reduce uncertainty, the less chance the client will have to resist. You can reduce uncertainty by being predictable. Deliver on your promises. Don't surprise the client.

One source of client uncertainty is the inability to understand what the result of your design will be. Clients may find it difficult to translate a two dimensional plan into a vision of a building or interior. Or they may not be able to comprehend what an interior will look like from a paint chip or fabric swatch. Find ways to help clients visualize the result and you will reduce their uncertainty.

Another way to reduce uncertainty is to increase trust. The more your clients trust you the less risk they perceive. The techniques described in the previous section on trust are extremely helpful in this regard.

There may be times, however, when you can't get past the resistance. It is important to recognize when you have reached that point and should let go. You can't make the client do something he or she doesn't want to do. It is better for both of you to accept the situation and part company than to continue battling each other.

When you do let go, you will earn the client's respect. The irony is that as soon as you do let go, the client usually ends the resistance: It is hard to resist when there is no one to resist back. At that point, you can decide whether you want to try to continue or make your decision final.

Recommended Reading

Ailes, Roger and Jon Kraushar, *You Are the Message*, Dow Jones-Irwin, Homewood, Illinois, 1988.

Block, Peter, *Flawless Consulting*, University Associates, San Diego, California, 1981.

Bramson, Robert M., *Coping With Difficult People*, Ballantine Books, New York, 1981.

Burley-Allen, Madelyn, *Listening*, John Wiley and Sons, New York, 1982.

Fisher, Roger and Scott Brown, *Getting Together*, Houghton Mifflin, Boston, 1988.

Fisher, Roger and William Urey, *Getting to YES*, Houghton Mifflin, Boston, 1981.

Laborde, Genie, *Influencing With Integrity*, Syntony Publishing, Palo Alto, California, 1987.

Weinberg, Gerald, *The Secrets of Consulting*, Dorset House, New York, 1985.

7
Working With Groups

The way you do things affects how well you do them. The method you use to make decisions determines, in part, how good the decisions will be. The processes you use to do projects significantly affects the results. If you understand the effect of the process on the product, you can design the situation to produce the highest-quality results.

That is as true of the way people interact as it is of the way projects are produced. Much of the work of a practice is done in groups. With an understanding of the interpersonal processes that occur within groups, you can act to improve group performance. Because of the pervasiveness of group activities in a practice, such improvement will have a substantial impact on the quality and quantity of the work you do.

Groups come about to do work that one person either cannot do or does not want to do alone. The natural focus in a design practice is on the project team, for that is where most effort is spent. But many other activities take place in a group setting: principals' meetings, coordinating the work of more than one project team, staff meetings, working with department or studio heads, and developing an associates' program. The practice itself is also a group.

This chapter begins with an examination of the impact of communication on group effectiveness. It then describes how groups develop and what you as a leader can do to facilitate their development. The balance of the chapter discusses problem solving and decision making, since much group activity is focused on those activities.

Communication and Group Effectiveness

Communication within the group is crucial to the group's success.[1] When participants communicate openly and effectively, they get more information and different points of view. That increases the chances that the group will do high quality work. When members communicate openly and have their viewpoints considered by the rest of the group, they are more likely to go along with and carry out the ultimate decision.

Patterns of participation are important. In most groups, some members are very vocal and others are more quiet. When they do speak, the quiet members usually talk less frequently and not as long as the others. In this situation, the vocal members often accuse the quiet ones of not contributing to the discussion. Quiet members, on the other hand, see it differently: They feel that no one has been listening to them.

When that happens, the quiet members feel rejected and tend to withdraw even more; they withhold their contributions from the group. That becomes a problem when a quiet member has information or skills that are necessary or helpful to the group. An important skill for you as a group leader, therefore, is to be able to encourage all group members to participate.

Interruptions are a common form of behavior in a group. When someone interrupts, it often means that the interrupter is more interested in what he or she thinks than in what others are saying. Frequent interruptions suggest that participants lack respect or concern for one another. The result is insufficient listening. Another skill of an effective group leader, then, is the ability to prevent interruptions and to enhance listening among the members.

People communicate in a variety of styles. They can be assertive, humorous, didactic, pompous, acerbic, or questioning. A common trap is for members of a group to pay more attention to how someone says something than to what the person says. That can seriously hinder communication and thereby reduce the effectiveness of the group. As a

---

[1] A more complete discussion of the effect of communication on the group and the development of the group is found in Edgar H. Schein, *Process Consultation*, 2nd ed., vol. 1, Addison-Wesley, Reading, Massachusetts, Chapters 4–6, pp. 40–83, 1988.

group leader, you need to be aware of how different communication styles affect participants and help members see beyond style to substance.

People communicate from different levels within themselves. When the different levels send the same message, the communication is clear. But when the different levels conflict with one another, the result is a mixed message. There are several levels of the self that are important in communication. The first consists of the parts of your personality you are aware of and are willing to share with others. It is called your *open self*.

The second is the *concealed self*, the parts of your personality you are aware of but don't want to share with others. They may deal with insecurities, anxieties, feelings that go against the prevailing norms, or feelings and reactions that might harm or hurt others or are just impolite. You may, for example, feel that a staff member working on a critical project is not performing at an appropriate level. But you may not say anything because you don't want to hurt the person or alienate him or her before the project is complete.

The third part of the self consists of things you are not consciously aware of but do communicate to other people. An example of this *blind self* in action is when you say you welcome feedback but react defensively to even the slightest criticism.

When two people communicate, each part of one person's self can interact with each part of the other person's self. Most communication is between people's open selves and is fairly straightforward. But there can be significant consequences when other parts of the self get involved, especially when the different parts contradict one another.

If one person operates from his open self and another from her blind self, the result can be mixed messages. The one operating from the blind self sends messages of which she is unaware. When the structural engineer says "I agree" with his jaw clenched and a constricted tone, his words say one thing but nonverbal cues give an entirely different meaning. Another situation is for one individual to communicate from his concealed self to the other's open self. The first person confides in the second, deliberately revealing something he might ordinarily conceal.

A less common situation, but no less important, is when one person's blind self communicates to another's blind self. In that case, A may influence B's feelings without either being aware of it. For example, a project manager may project anxiety even though he or she denies being tense. The members of the team may then pick up on the anxiety without being aware of the source of their own feelings. Or they may become tense because they don't know whether to respond to the manager's denial or to the anxiety. In either case, they feel anxious without knowing why.

Understanding the dynamics of communication between the various levels of the self will help you be a better group leader. It will help you understand what is happening within the group and suggest ways to enhance its functioning. You may see the need to open channels that might not otherwise be available. For example, you might decide that the team's effectiveness would improve if you could get people to confide in each other more. Or you could conclude that one member's hidden feelings were hindering his or her ability to contribute to the project.

Your goal as group leader is to get the most out of the group. If improving communications will make the group's work better or easier, that's what you need to do. You also need to consider the cost of not communicating. What would happen if, for example, some members decided not to express their opposition to an idea or proposal? Would that lead them to resist implementation? On the other hand, if people are too open, could that make them vulnerable in some harmful way?

How Groups Evolve

As a group such as a project team or office staff forms, grows, and matures, it moves through a series of developmental stages. At each stage, members address a distinctive set of issues. Only after resolving those issues successfully can the group achieve maximum effectiveness. It is important for you to recognize the stages of development and allow for them. The group needs time to build itself into a team. If that process doesn't occur, it could inhibit the group's development and adversely affect the quality of its work.

Groups develop on two levels. The first is task behavior: the actual work the group is supposed to do. The second level is group process: the way the members work together as a group. The more effectively the members can work together, the more successful they will be in their work.

When people come together in a new group, their first concern is with individual issues; members want to know how they will fit in. Only after they resolve those issues will they pay more attention to each other and to the job. Their first concern is identity: the role they will play in the group process. Some people choose to be dominant, assertive, and task-oriented. Others concentrate on the social or emotional aspects of the group, such as relieving tension or encouraging everyone to participate. Usually people are comfortable when they concentrate on one aspect or the other; occasionally one individual will take on both aspects.

One factor that influences a person's choice of role in the group is the formal job assignment. The project manager or client representative is expected to act in a certain way on the project team — that's his or her job. Another factor is experience. A person looks at the current situation and decides his or her role in terms of what has worked in the past. Until the issue is resolved, identity will be a source of anxiety and tension. Those feelings will focus attention inward rather than on what is happening within the group. The person will listen less, pay less attention, and contribute less to the group's effort.

Another initial concern of members is how power and influence are distributed within the group. People have their own needs in this area, whether they have to do with the actual work, methods, group processes, prominence, or position within the group. At first — especially if they haven't worked with each other before — members don't know each others' needs or styles. As a result, they spend time testing each other, trying things out, jockeying for position. That is a period of getting acquainted. When things finally are sorted out, members become more comfortable with and accepting of the situation. Then they can turn their attention to the tasks of the group.

Each member has an agenda of individual needs and desires. He or she wants to know whether and how the group can meet them. That concern may cause individuals to withhold their investment in the group until they get a clearer picture of what they can get from the group. If too many members hold back, it may be difficult to get the group going. The leader can impose goals and provide an agenda for the group, but that doesn't ensure individual commitment.

When members see that they can meet their personal goals through the group, they will have greater commitment to group goals. A good strategy for accomplishing that is to incorporate goals of individual members, as far as possible, into the goals of the group. One architecture and engineering firm does that by having its project managers at the first meeting of the project team ask members what they want from the project. One individual, for example, might wish to get certain types of experience or learn new skills. The project manager uses such information to develop a plan that encompasses individual goals within the work of the group.

The final set of issues in this initial stage of group development involves questions of acceptance and intimacy. Members want to know whether they will be liked and accepted by others; they also want to figure out how close to others they must be for it to happen.

There are no rules of thumb for resolving those issues; every group determines its own standards. Among the questions they must answer are these: how members address each other; how polite people must be to one another; how formal or informal the operating procedures will be; and when the group must stay with its formal task and when it will allow personal exchanges.

Every new group, every new project team must go through this process of development before it can function effectively. Every new member must deal with these issues before he or she can fully participate. When people have worked together before, the group will move more quickly through this stage of development. However, even in such a group these issues must be confronted when new members are added to the mix.

Groups need time to build themselves. As a group leader, you must be patient enough to give the group time to develop into a team. Recognize that initial anger, tension, and impatience are indications that development is taking place.

Over time, members begin to understand how the others in the group feel and react. They realize that they can fit into the group and contribute to it. Then they can relax and focus more of their attention on others and on the task. The mood of the group changes; the group becomes a team. This transformation happens, however, only when the group is allowed to work out its problems. The members must do it themselves. Solutions can't be imposed—by a group leader or anyone else—without affecting the ultimate effectiveness of the team.

How Groups Function

After the group has solved the initial problems, it carries out three kinds of functions. The first set has to do with the task itself; the second involves building and maintaining good relations within the group, and the third has to do with how the group responds to external forces.

Tasks—the Work of the Group

The first set of functions, the one that involves the actual work of the group, can vary from taking one or more steps in the design process to developing operational procedures for the office to creating a strategic plan. The first task function is to get the group working. Someone needs to describe the problem the group is to work on, define the goal, suggest how to proceed, and set targets. When a group first forms, this *initiating* role comes from the group leader—the project manager, the principal in charge, or the committee chair. As the group develops, members themselves can take on this function.

Once the problem is defined and the goal is set, the group needs to *gather information and form opinions* as a basis for making decisions. Since the quality of information directly affects the quality of the solution, the group needs to spend enough time gathering information. One common trap is to spend too little time at this stage. It also is important to distinguish between fact and opinion.

As information gets to the group, members need to *clarify and elaborate* on the information to make sure they really understand it. Doing so also gives members an opportunity to build on each others' ideas as a way to stimulate creativity.

One way to ensure that ideas aren't lost and that everyone is at the same point in the process is to *summarize*. Review the points that have been discussed and the ideas that people have put forth. A good time to do that is when the group is ready to make a decision; that way, all the members can have full information before they decide. Summarizing also enables the group to step back from the details and look at the broader perspective.

You can summarize the discussion yourself, or you can ask someone else to put the major points on a blackboard or flip chart. Another way is to ask someone to review what he or she has heard and then draw tentative conclusions for the group to consider.

When you are ready to decide, it is a good idea to check whether the members agree or want additional time for discussion. Timing is important. On the one hand, if some members feel that the decision is premature, they might feel they were steamrollered. That could affect their subsequent contributions. On the other hand, if the decision drags on too long, some members might feel frustrated and dissatisfied.

Maintaining Good Relations

Besides doing the work of the group, members need to build and maintain good relationships within the group. A member of the team who doesn't have a positive relationship with others, becomes preoccupied with personal feelings and is less able to contribute to the group. Maintenance activities help prevent or repair damaged relationships so members can again focus their attention on the group's work.

Group Functions

Task functions

Integrating
Giving and gathering information and opinion
Clarifying
Elaborating
Summarizing
Deciding

Maintenance functions

Gatekeeping
Encouraging
Harmonizing
Compromising
Setting and testing standards

Boundary functions

Defining boundaries
Monitoring
Negotiating
Guarding
Managing entry and exit

The *gatekeeping* function gives people who have something to say the opportunity to make a contribution. It is a way to get passive or quiet members involved in the discussion. It also helps to prevent interruptions, which can be destructive to group effectiveness.

Encouragement assists someone who is having difficulty making a point; it helps both the group and the member. The group hears the point the member is trying to make, and the member gains acceptance.

Healthy conflict and disagreement stimulate creativity and promote integrative solutions. If people who disagree can devise a solution that takes into account their differing views, they may be able to come up with a better decision than could be otherwise obtained. Destructive disagreement, however, can hurt relationships. When that happens, *harmonizing and compromising* help repair the damage. (Though these functions are often used in group problem solving, they have only limited usefulness in that capacity.)

Periodically, the group should take time out from its work to look at how it functions. Only by paying attention to its process can the group improve the way it works. That is especially true if the group is losing its effectiveness. Ask members how they feel about the group; have them examine how the group is operating; ask them to describe the group's problems and conflicts.

Boundary Functions

Every group functions within a larger environment. A project team exists within a studio or department; a studio exists within a practice. Even in smaller practices there may be more than one project team. Important functions occur at the boundary between the group and its external environment.

Every group has to define itself, to determine who belongs and who doesn't. Often, membership in a group is designated. Project teams, studios, departments, and formal task forces operate that way. Yet even formal groups have to define themselves: Is a person who is temporarily assigned to a project team treated the same way as a permanent member?

However a group defines itself, it acts to maintain its own integrity. The group can be exclusive or inclusive, open or closed. Several issues come into play: Who can come to its meetings. What information should be shared with others outside the group and what should be kept confidential. How new members are brought into the group. What happens when a current member leaves.

No group is entirely self-sufficient; every group needs information and resources from the larger environment. A project team wants to know what resources are available to it, what people think of it, and what its future is. To ensure that it has the resources necessary to function effectively, the group negotiates with outside people and groups. That is what happens when a project manager requests additional people or time to complete a particular phase of the project.

Communication between the group and the external environment needs translation. The group must both interpret the messages from the environment and decide what it wants to say to people on the outside.

By being aware of the functions of the group process, you can design them to enhance the group's performance rather than hinder it. The group can and should monitor its own process. You can do that at each meeting or each week, depending on the nature of the group. Begin with an open-ended discussion about how well the group is functioning. As the group becomes more aware of its process and more sophisticated, you can use a diagnostic survey such as the one shown in Figure 7.1. You can ask group members individually to complete the survey, analyze the results, and then discuss the results during one of the meetings.

Figure 7.1. Criteria of group maturity. (*Edgar Schein*, Process Consultation, *vol. 1*, © 1988. Reprinted by permission of Addison-Wesley Publishing Co., Inc., Reading, Massachusetts.)

1. Adequate mechanisms for getting feedback:

   | Poor feedback mechanisms | 1 | 2 | 3 | 4 | 5 | Excellent feedback mechanisms |

   Average

2. Adequate decision-making procedure:

   | Poor decision-making procedure | 1 | 2 | 3 | 4 | 5 | Very adequate decision-making procedure |

   Average

3. Optimal cohesion:

   | Low cohesion | 1 | 2 | 3 | 4 | 5 | Optimal cohesion |

   Average

4. Flexible organization and procedures:

   | Very flexible | 1 | 2 | 3 | 4 | 5 | Very flexible |

   Average

5. Maximum use of member resources:

   | Poor use of resources | 1 | 2 | 3 | 4 | 5 | Excellent use of resources |

   Average

6. Clear communications:

   | Poor communication | 1 | 2 | 3 | 4 | 5 | Excellent communication |

   Average

7. Clear goals accepted by members:

   | Unclear goals — not accepted | 1 | 2 | 3 | 4 | 5 | Very clear goals — accepted |

   Average

(Continued)

Figure 7.1. Criteria of group maturity. (*Continued*)

8. Feelings of interdependence with authority persons:

No inter-   1   2   3   4   5   High interdependence   _____   dependence
                    Average

9. Shared participation in leadership functions:

No shared   1   2   3   4   5   High shared
participation _____   participation
                    Average

10. Acceptance of minority views and persons:

No accep-   1   2   3   4   5   High acceptance
tance   _____
                    Average

Group Norms

Behavior in the early stages of a group's development sets precedents for future behavior. When, for example, one member confronts another, the way the group responds establishes a standard for openness and confrontation. Or take another case: In the initial meeting of the project team, the designer disagrees publicly with the project manager. The project manager reacts negatively—with criticism and possibly censure. The response signals the other members that in the future the project manager wants his or her suggestions to be taken as orders.

When patterns of behavior persist, they become norms. Norms are sets of assumptions or expectations that members share about what kind of behavior is right or wrong, good or bad, permitted or forbidden. Most often, norms are unspoken and implicit. They are not easy to identify or to define because they operate deep within people's minds, invisibly, as personal guidelines. But they are extremely influential in determining how members behave, how they perceive things, and how they feel.

Because they operate below the level of awareness, norms are tricky. A common trap for a group is to assume that a norm is operating when, in fact, there is no agreement. In such situations, people withhold their own opinions and ideas, which they feel will be rejected because they run counter to the supposed norm. Anyone who challenged the assumption could prove it wrong. But because everyone makes an assumption that isn't so, the members do something that no one really wants.

Norms can be explicit—either spoken or written. When someone says "that's the way we do it here" he or she is passing on a norm of the firm.

At Gensler and Associates, for example, the phrase "the Gensler way" is shorthand for a compilation of the norms of behavior that are followed in that practice.

Just because something is written doesn't mean that it operates as a norm. There is a significant difference between a written policy in an office manual and a norm. If the written policy is enforced in practice and reinforced in behavior, it is a true norm. Otherwise, it is merely a pious platitude that lacks real influence over the way people act.

As a principal, you can establish the norms of the practice. As a group leader, you must be aware of the norms that are active and evaluate whether they are appropriate and effective. If they are not, you can try to change them, but that is a long and difficult task. One factor complicating such an effort is that multiple norms may be in force simultaneously. They may either support or contradict one another. If you want to change one, you must to change all.

For example, assume that the group has developed the norm that everyone must do as the project manager asks. This norm is supported by others, such as "one mustn't disagree publicly with the project manager," and "one mustn't speak out if one disagrees with the decision that is being made." To change the decision norm to seek consensus on important decisions, it is also necessary to change people's attitudes on participation and disagreement.

Relationships Between Groups

In all but the smallest practices several groups exist simultaneously; the larger the practice the more groups there are. There may be a design group and a technical group, a group of professionals and a support staff, a studio A group and a studio B group. Each group develops its own loyalties, norms, values, and goals within the context of the practice.

Groups can coexist cooperatively as well as competitively. Because of the prevailing values of our culture, there is a tendency to encourage competitiveness among groups to motivate the groups to be more effective and productive. But competitiveness may be counterproductive in both the short and long term. Competition does not necessarily improve the quality of the solutions; in fact, quality may be sacrificed in order to win. Competition can be especially harmful when two groups, such as a design department and a production department, depend on one another.

Problems arise if competition creates a win-lose situation. At first, the individual groups draw together. They tighten their structures; they concentrate on their tasks; and they pay less attention to the needs of the members.

As the team gets more cohesive, the competition becomes the enemy. Its view of the world becomes increasingly black and white; it sees only its own strengths, not its weaknesses, and it sees the other group primarily in negative terms. Hostility increases. Interaction and communication between the two groups diminish, reinforcing the groups' negative views of one another. When the two groups do interact, each tends to pay attention only to its own view and not listen to or consider the other's. Instead of interchange between the two groups being stimulated, competition has stifled it. Each group is limited in what it can learn from the other.

Winning can be beneficial for the winners. They can build on their accomplishments and become even more successful. But they can also become complacent. They can release the tension that the competition has created and lose their focus and spirit.

Losers, on the other hand, suffer the effects of losing. They may try to deny that they lost, or they may engage in scapegoating. The group can splinter and lose its cohesiveness, or it can refocus on the task and look for a positive direction. From its loss, it can learn about how it works and why it fell short. If it can continue to learn, it can regroup to compete again.

It is easier to prevent these problems from happening than to correct them once they have occurred. You can deemphasize or limit competition. You can monitor the situation to make sure that competition doesn't get out of hand. You can create a cooperative situation in which both (or all) groups win because people tend to do better when there are cooperative rather than competing goals.

Group Problem Solving and the Design Process

Solving problems is a basic activity of every work group. When a project team develops a realistic schedule and budget for the project or develops the best design for a building, space, or interior, it is solving problems. When principals devise a marketing plan or operating policies, they are solving problems. When a task force formulates a set of values for the practice, it, too, is solving problems.

The process of problem solving is the same whether the problem is in design, finance, business, or marketing. As Dan Dworsky stated, "I see the problem-solving process very clearly in relation to the design process. Intellectually they are the same process." Table 7.1 shows the parallels between problem solving and the design process. But when a

Table 7.1. Problem Solving and the Design Process.

Steps in the design process	Steps in problem solving
Acceptance	Sense and recognize a need
Analysis	Diagnose the problem Analyze the problem
Definition	Define the problem Define decision criteria
Ideation	Generate alternative solutions
Selection	Test and evaluate alternatives Select a solution
Implementation	Plan action steps Take action
Evaluation	Control and follow-up Evaluation

group is involved, you need to be sensitive to the interaction between group process and the problem-solving process.

When you design a space or a building, the client brings you the problem. But before you can solve a problem in your practice, you must first acknowledge that one exists. Your first awareness of a problem is of symptoms: You are not getting enough clients; you are not making enough money; you are not getting the kinds of projects you want. As symptoms accumulate, they pass a threshold of recognition. They cause you to become aware that something is wrong or that something must be improved. That recognition is the first step in the process: *acceptance*.

Now you need to distinguish between the symptoms and the underlying problem; you need to look for possible sources. This is the *analysis* step, in which you define the limits of the problem. Since the way you identify the real problem determines the nature and quality of the solution, this is the most critical stage.

As an illustration, assume that one of your partners tells you that the staff is complaining about excessive overtime. He or she maintains that it is because the new people just don't have the same dedication and work ethic as the principals do. What your partner is really saying is that something is happening to cause people to feel tense and frustrated. The issue "lack of commitment" is just a convenient name for the source of these feelings. Chances are that at this point your partner hasn't systematically examined the situation to get a real understanding of the true problem.

One way to approach this problem is to gather data. See if others have heard the same complaints and have the same perception about commitment. Find out from time cards the average number of hours people actually work in a week. Get concrete examples of overtime and critical incidents when scheduling has been a problem. Ask staff about their concerns about overtime and their feelings about the causes. If the information is not readily available, figure out how to get it.

Once you have the data, you can begin to diagnose the source. Is there a relation between the complaints and the amount of overtime? How often do you get complaints? Does overtime occur on every project or just on particular types? Does it happen at every stage of the project or only in particular phases? Look for patterns and relationships; try to understand each aspect of the problem and how it relates to the whole.

Your analysis of the patterns of overtime and complaints should give you clues about the sources. These hints enable you to distill your understanding of the situation into an explanation of the nature of the problem. The *definition* of the problem should also include criteria and guidelines for eventual solutions.

You may find out that the people who are most concerned about overtime are new employees, who don't have the experience and values of those who have been with the practice longer. You also may decide that another source of the problem is an inadequate system for scheduling projects. By defining the problem in this way, you are saying that any solution must address the issue of cultivating the values of the practice in all employees as well as improve the scheduling procedures.

Now that the problem is defined, the group can begin to generate ideas to resolve it. This is the *ideation* stage. One method that is useful in generating solutions is the *nominal group technique*.[2] After posing a question to the group, the members jot down ideas individually, without any discussion. After 10 minutes, individual members give their ideas one at a time in a round robin. The ideas are jotted on a flip chart by a facilitator. The only discussion permitted at this time is a request for clarification. Participants are encouraged to hitchhike on one another's ideas. Members continue giving their ideas until no one has any more. This technique is particularly effective in getting everyone to participate in the process.

The next step is *selection*: choosing the best alternative you have generated. That requires you to assess the solutions with the criteria you specified in the definition stage above. A common pitfall at this step is to look at proposed solutions one at a time instead of evaluating an en-

[2] For a more complete discussion of the nominal group technique see Andre Delbecq, Andy Vandeven, and D. Gustafsen, *Group Techniques for Program Planning*, Scott, Foresman, Glenview, Illinois, 1975.

tire range of possible solutions. Because you haven't compared solutions to one another, you can't develop the perspective that is critical to developing high-quality solutions. You take the first one that makes sense, instead of attempting to come up with solutions that might offer even more advantages. Another consequence is that the person who offers the idea may feel personally judged as well. If he feels rejected, he might withdraw from the process or be reluctant to contribute later.

At this stage, the group moves from planning to *implementation*. Having chosen an alternative, it has to plan its actions and carry them out. You can use the process described above to plan your action. The problem to be solved now becomes the best way to carry out the solution. By using the same steps, the group can generate alternative ways to implement the solution and select the best among the options.

Having planned the action, the group has to make sure that it is carried out. One way to do so is to assign specific responsibilities to specific people to carry out by a specific time. If the people who implement the solution are different from those who devised it, you may run into problems. Since the implementers haven't gone through the process, they may not fully understand the thinking behind the solution. They may have reservations about the solution and therefore be less committed. They may have different perspectives, or they may see or know things that the first group did not know or that they missed.

You can avoid these problems by involving the implementers as early in the cycle as possible. Ideally, they should participate in the planning. That way, they can participate in the process and contribute their viewpoints to the solution. That is why it is a good policy to include project managers early in the discussions with a client.

The last step in the problem solving process, and the step most often ignored, is *evaluation*. Evaluation tells you how well you did in solving the problem and how well your problem-solving process worked. It provides a systematic means by which the practice can learn from its experience. Your evaluation may highlight deficiencies in the earlier stages. For example, it may indicate that your initial definition of the problem was mistaken. The information can help you improve both the solution and the process the next time.

Decisions

Which is the best way to make a decision depends on a number of factors. Though there is no one right way, some ways are more appropriate than others in certain situations. And the particular way you choose will affect the quality of decision you make.

Two writers, Victor Vroom and Philip Yetton, have developed a model that can help you determine what your alternatives are.[3] You can make the decision yourself, consult with your subordinates for ideas and suggestions before making the decision yourself, or let the group make the decision. Vroom and Yetton define five decision styles:

AI. You solve the problem or make the decision yourself, by using information available to you at the time. No one else is involved.

AII. You get the necessary information from others (subordinates, consultants, clients), but you make the decision yourself. When you ask for information, you may or may not tell the others why you need it or what the problem is. The involvement of the others is limited to providing necessary information to you, rather than generating or evaluating alternative solutions.

CI. You discuss the problem with other people individually. You get their ideas and suggestions without bringing them together as a group. The decision, which you make yourself, may or may not reflect the influence of the other people.

CII. You share the problem with others as a group, collectively obtaining their ideas and suggestions. You then make the decision, which may or may not reflect the influence of the others.

GII. You share a problem with others as a group. Together you generate and evaluate alternatives and attempt to reach agreement on a solution. You do not try to influence the group to adopt "your" solution, and you are willing to accept and carry out any solution that has the support of the entire group.

The appropriate style depends on several factors. Vroom and Yetton provide seven "diagnostic questions" the answers to which help narrow down the decision styles that are appropriate:

A. *Is quality important in the decision?* A positive answer means that one alternative is likely to be better than the others. For example, is one design solution better than the others? Does one design cost more to build than another? If a high-quality decision is important, the leader has to be actively involved.

B. *Do you have enough information or expertise to make a high quality decision by yourself?* If you as leader don't have the ability or facts to assess the quality of each alternative, you need to involve others to get that information.

---

[3]The decision model is found in Victor H. Vroom and Philip W. Yetton, *Leadership and Decision-Making*, University of Pittsburgh, Pittsburgh, Pennsylvania, 1973.

C. *Is the problem well structured?* In a structured problem, the leader knows what information is needed and where to get it. In an unstructured problem, the problem is ambiguous and there are no clear procedures for solving it. When a problem is unstructured, the leader will usually need to interact with others to clarify it and come up with alternative solutions.

D. *Is it important that others accept the decision in order to carry it out effectively?* If success requires that the people who have to implement the decision agree with it, acceptance is important. In such a situation, you should involve those who will implement the decision in the process.

E. *If you make the decision yourself, will the others in the group accept it?* If the group members always accept your decision, their involvement is less important.

F. *Is a mutually acceptable solution likely?* If the members of the group share the same goals and values, you can create a win-win situation and use a problem-solving approach. If not, there will be conflict and the matter will be settled based on power.

G. *Will members of the group be in conflict over the proposed solution?* If a disagreement is likely, you should allow members to participate in the discussion.

These questions quickly narrow the options and lead to the appropriate level of group participation in the decision. The flowchart in Figure 7.2 summarizes the process. Start on the left side of the chart with question 1 and answer each question with yes or no. Proceed until you come to the number that tells you the problem type and the appropriate decision style. The feasible methods are shown in Table 7.2.

Once you determine the problem type, you still have to decide which of the styles you will use. If the problem is type 1, for example, and efficiency is your main concern, make the decision yourself. However, your practice may have a value that stresses staff involvement, and in that case you should include staff members in the decision.

To illustrate how the model works, take an actual example. In a medium-size architectural practice, the project managers have been complaining that they have too much to do and too little time in which to do it. Problems in the scheduling of both projects and people exacerbate the situation. Projects seem to cluster; they reach the same phases simultaneously and cause the work flow to go up and down like a roller coaster. The situation is preventing staff members from being effective in their jobs. The people involved most directly are the two principals and three project managers. Each of them has some informa-

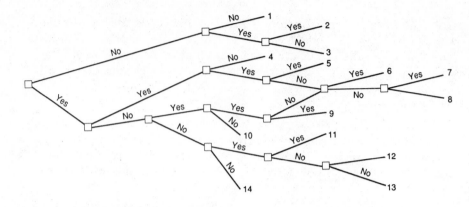

A. Is there a requirement such that one solution is likely to be more rational than another?
B. Do I have sufficient information to make a high-quality decision?
C. Is the problem structured?
D. Is acceptance of decision by subordinates critical to effective implementation?
E. If I were to make the decision by myself, it is reasonably certain that it would be accepted by my subordinates?
F. Is a mutually acceptable solution likely?
G. Is conflict among subordinates likely in preferred solutions?

Figure 7.2. Decision process flowchart. (*Reprinted from* Leadership and Decision-making, *by Victor H. Vroom and Philip W. Yetton, by permission of the University of Pittsburgh Press © 1973.*)

Table 7.2. Problem Types and the Feasible Set of Decision Processes.

Problem type	Acceptable methods
1.	AI, AII, CI, CII, GII
2.	AI, AII, CI, CII, GII
3.	GII
4.	AI, AII, CI, CII, GII°
5.	AI, AII, CI, CII, GII°
6.	GII
7.	CII
8.	CI, CII
9.	AII, CI, CII, GII°
10.	AII, CI, CII, GII°
11.	CII, GII°
12.	GII
13.	CII
14.	CII, GII°

°Within the feasible set only when the answer to question F is yes.

Reprinted from *Leadership and Decision-Making*, by Victor H. Vroom and Philip W. Yetton, by permission of the University of Pittsburgh Press © 1973.

tion to contribute to an understanding of the problem, but no one has all the answers to the problem.

When the questions in the Vroom-Yetton model were posed, the following answers were given:

A. Is there a quality factor?   Yes

B. Do you (the principal) have enough information to make the decision yourself?   No

C. Is the problem structured?   No

D. Is acceptance of the decision by subordinates critical to implementation?   No

This problem is type 14, Table 7.2. In this case, the principal should either call a meeting to get suggestions or solutions (CII) or use a group problem-solving technique (GII).

Methods of Making Decisions in Groups

If the group will participate in the decision, you need to establish how they will do it. There are a number of ways in which the group can proceed.[4] Again, your choice depends on such factors as the amount of time you have to make the decision, the kind of decision you are making, the history of the group, and the values of your practice.

1. *The group decides by inaction or by lack of response.* In this method, someone comes up with the first idea. The group discusses it for a while until someone else introduces a second proposal. Another suggestion is floated and then another until the group finds one alternative it can agree on. By using this method, the group decides by not deciding, passing over ideas it doesn't support.

2. *The chair of the group makes the decision.* This is the most efficient method. It is effective if the leader is sensitive to the needs of the members, listens well, and has a good sense of when it is appropriate to make the decision. It also allows the least opportunity for group involvement. Because members are not involved, they may have less commitment to carry out the ultimate decision.

---

[4] For a fuller discussion of group decision-making methods see Edgar H. Schein, *Process Consultation*, 2nd ed., vol. 1, Addison-Wesley, Reading, Massachusetts, pp. 69–75, 1988.

3. *The minority decides.* This is the case when an individual or a subgroup takes actions that present the group with a fait accompli without the consent of the majority or when one or two people railroad a decision through. Leaders often allow this to happen because they mistake the group's silence to mean consent. A lack of response may mean that members feel pressure to conform or sense that any disagreement will be seen as obstructionist behavior.

4. *Majority rules.* This is the most common form of group decision making: Action is taken either by a formal vote or an informal poll. Although it can be an efficient method, it has several drawbacks that could make the implementation of decisions ineffective. If minority members feel they didn't have a sufficient chance to discuss their views or even to get their views considered, they may feel misunderstood and rejected. Alternatively, the minority may feel that the vote was a power contest that they lost. That may lead them to hold back and regroup until they can win enough support for their views. In either case, the focus is on winning, and not on solving the problem. To get the most out of voting, you must develop ways to have members commit to the ultimate decision whether or not their side wins.

5. *The group reaches a consensus.* This is the most effective decision method—and the most time-consuming. Consensus exists when the group develops an option that most members support. Those not in favor feel they have had an adequate opportunity to make their case; they understand the majority position and are willing to support it. Consensus is different from unanimity. In a unanimous decision, members may vote for a solution they do not support if they feel enough pressure to conform. In a consensus decision, members may vote against a solution but are committed to its implementation because they feel they have had a fair hearing.

Because it is so time-consuming, consensus should be used mainly for significant decisions that require maximum commitment from the group. For example, you can use it to determine which kinds of decisions will be decided by which method.

If you want all the group members to be actively involved in the discussion and reach consensus, a smaller group is more effective. The ideal group size for this kind of task is five or seven. A group of two is least desirable because either party can withdraw if he or she feels rejected. Three is almost as bad because there can be coalitions of two against one. With four or six people, you can be stalemated. With five or seven members, if coalitions are formed, the dissenters usually have company. When groups get larger than seven, they tend to become fragmented and formal, and people participate less. Larger groups need a more structured process to insure that everyone has a chance to have his or her ideas considered.

Recommended Reading

Delbecq, Andre, Andy Vandeven, and D. Gustafson, *Group Techniques for Program Planning*, Scott, Foresman, Glenview, Illinois, 1975.

Filley, Alan C., *The Compleat Manager*, Green Briar Press, Middleton, Wisconsin, 1978.

Koberg, Don and Jim Bagnall, *The Universal Traveler*, revised, William Kaufmann, Inc., Los Altos, California, 1981.

Russo, J. Edward and Paul J. H. Schoemaker, *Decision Traps*, Doubleday, New York, 1989.

Schein, Edgar H., *Process Consultation*, 2nd ed., vol. 1, Addison-Wesley, Reading, Massachusetts, 1988.

Vroom, Victor H. and Philip W. Yetton, *Leadership and Decision-Making*, University of Pittsburgh Press, Pittsburgh, Pennsylvania, 1973.

PART 3

Making It Happen

8

Personal Effectiveness

Things happen in time: Time is measured by the occurrence of events one after another. The events can be acts, thoughts, ideas, or feelings. They can be random, or they can be controlled. When you manage a sequence of events to accomplish a goal, you have used your time effectively.

Time is an equal-opportunity resource. Everyone has the same amount—you have neither more nor less than anyone else. That some people seem to have more time than others merely shows that they know how to manage time more successfully. Time is also your most predictable resource. You always know how much you have. Best of all, it doesn't cost you anything.

The issue is not whether you have the time; it is how you use the time you have. Principals who practice by design are masters of time. They know how to harness its power in the pursuit of their goals.

Thinking About Time

When you are caught in traffic on your way to a client meeting, nothing you can do will get you there any sooner. All you can do is take steps to cope with the traffic: You can anticipate traffic problems by leaving a few minutes early; you can use the driving time productively by listening to tapes or by using a minicassette recorder to make notes or dictate messages; or you can install a cellular phone to conduct business or call ahead to say you will be late. But if there is a traffic jam, you are stuck.

Knowing the limits of your influence is the first key to effective use of time. You can manage only the things over which you have control.[1] Certain events are plainly beyond your control: the economy, floods, droughts, and earthquakes. Trying to control those events is a prescription for frustration, anger, and futility. The best and healthiest approach is to accept them and prepare for their consequences.

Another type of event is the one you think you can control but, in fact, can't. When you try to control such an event, whether out of naïveté or arrogance, you are doomed to failure. Not only do you risk losing confidence in yourself, you also waste time, energy, and other resources.

For example, you can't control a client's reaction to your ideas, but you can control your own actions in ways that may influence the outcome. You can thoroughly research and prepare your proposals so they meet his or her concerns and desires. You can prepare alternatives instead of just giving your client one idea to consider. And you can help a client identify the source of his or her resistance so you can develop a solution that will gain approval.

You can influence many events, but having control is different from exerting control. There are some events that you know you can control but don't. Those are the situations in which you are passive, lack the discipline to exercise your will, or become indecisive in the face of conflicting goals. A common example is when you have to reprimand or fire an employee. Most people don't like to do it so they don't act at all.

There are other events you think you cannot control but, in fact, you can. Those are circumstances in which you lose your nerve and fail to assert yourself. Examples are the myriad ways in which people waste time. Most people think that the causes of time waste are external. Upon reflection, however, they usually discover that the root causes are their own attitudes and actions.

Finally, there are events that you know you can control, and you do. Those are the situations in which you effectively use your time to accomplish your goals. The successes give you feelings of power and self-confidence.

The distinction between what you can and can't control is crucial. It allows you to take responsibility for that which is appropriately yours and to free yourself from unnecessary pressures. It also enables you to concentrate your energy where it can most effectively advance your goals.

---

[1] The notions of control over events are based upon the work of Charles R. Hobbs, *Your Time and Your Life: Insight System for Planning*, Nightengale-Conant Corp., Chicago, 1983 (sound cassette), and Robert J. Kriegel and Marilyn Harris Kriegel, *The C Zone*, Ballantine, New York, 1984.

Goals and Priorities

Time management is planning applied to daily activities. In planning, you have to know the direction in which you are going in order to get there. In time management, the same thing is true: you need to know what you want to accomplish so you can concentrate your time on getting it. Goals are statements of what you want to accomplish. They make the purposes of the practice explicit. By stating what is important to you, they serve as theoretical priorities.[2]

You always act with intent. You use time to get something, whether or not you are consciously aware of your purpose. Your behavior in practice—what you actually choose to do with your time—reveals your operational priorities. Success in time management is using your time to achieve your purpose. But reality often differs from theory: your theoretical priorities don't always match your operational priorities, and there is a gap between what you say you want to do and the way you use your time.

Before you can close the gap, you need to find out if it even exists. You need to become aware of your time behavior. That you do by keeping a time log: gathering data on what you do with your time. Keep track of your time for a minimum of three days and up to a week, including at least one non-workday. Monitor your activities from at least 7:00 a.m. to 9:00 p.m. It is important to get information on both professional and personal time to get an adequate indication of your priorities.

Note your activities every 15 minutes unless you are deeply involved in a task that requires uninterrupted concentration. For each segment, report all significant activities in terms of both the action and the result. Record your actions right away. If you wait too long, you may risk losing the details of your actions. Worse, you might adapt the record to what you wish had happened instead of what actually occurred. For the time log to be effective, you must not engage in wishful thinking.

With that information you can begin to analyze your use of time. First, compare the *is*—your operational priorities—with the *should*—your theoretical priorities. How much time do you actually spend in activities that directly contribute to your stated priorities? How much time do you spend in activities that are unrelated to them? If you discover a difference between the two, you need to figure out why it exists and take steps to reduce it. You can do that in one of two ways: Either change your behavior or change your goals.

---

[2]Theoretical and operational priorities are discussed at greater length in Jane Elizabeth Allen, *Beyond Time Management*, Addison-Wesley, Reading, Massachusetts, pp. 33–80, 1986.

If you find you are using your time for a purpose different from your stated goals, examine what it is you are getting out of those activities. What are they accomplishing? What functions are they serving? How important are they compared to your stated goals? Look at the goal that is not being met. If it is still valid, can you define it in another way, one that accommodates your behavior?

Assume that your firm has decided to increase its emphasis on design excellence. As design partner, your goal is to devote most of your time to design issues. However, your time log shows that you spend only 25 percent of your time in that activity.

On examining the situation, you find several reasons for your behavior. First, clients want you to be personally involved in supervising their projects. Second, your staff isn't adequately trained to handle your responsibilities so you can be free to do more design. Third, your staff is resisting the change because it threatens the status quo and you are not yet prepared to deal with that resistance.

Though your behavior is not focused on the stated goal of design excellence, it does accomplish other purposes. It keeps your clients satisfied, keeps the practice productive, and protects the staff from controversy and uncertainty. On the basis of your analysis, you decide that these are important goals, that they are equal in significance to design excellence. You conclude that the way to achieve your original goal is to spend time preparing your clients for the change, training your staff to take over your responsibilities, and developing a plan to reduce staff resistance.

Your goals and priorities don't always fit together in a neat little package. Though related, each is separate and distinct. Your goals may be constant, but your priorities are constantly changing. Some will be more critical at one time and less so at another. Be attuned to this competition so you can direct your attention appropriately.

Planning Your Day

Chapter 2 described how time spent on planning saves time in implementation. The same principle holds true in time management. Taking time each day to plan your activities accomplishes several purposes. You gather all the information you need about the things you need to do. You evaluate activities and assign priorities. And you focus your thinking and energy for the day so you can be more productive.

Some people prefer to allot 10 to 15 minutes first thing in the morning to planning. They feel that it centers them and prepares them for the rest of the day. Others like to set aside time in the late afternoon or evening so they can digest what has happened and consider the next day under less stress than would be the case in the morning. They then feel ready when they come to work.

Whenever you plan, the first step is to develop a to-do list. The items can be consolidated from notes you have on various projects, things you have to do with various people, and actions you want to take relating to your goals. Once you have the list, you must evaluate the items according to their priority for that day.

Priority is a function of both importance and urgency. The distinction is critical. Things are important to the extent that they get you toward your goal and have a significant payoff in terms of your priorities. Things are urgent when they have to be done immediately. Urgency and importance are independent attributes. Just because something has to be done now does not necessarily mean that it is just as important as a task that isn't due until next week. Use the following scale to rate an item's importance:

A	Extremely important	Items that have the highest payoff for priority goals
B	Important	Items that have a substantial payoff for priority goals
C	Not important or routine	Items that have average or less payoff

Next, assess each item on the list for its urgency. Some people merely identify items as either urgent or not urgent. Others have three categories:

Immediate	Things that need to be done within 24 hours
Soon	Things that need to be done within 7 days
Anytime	Things you need or want to do but have no deadline for doing

If those criteria do not fit with the way you work, you may wish to develop others. But write them down so they become concrete guidelines for consistency. Here are some additional questions that may help you establish priorities:

- Which of my goals should I work on today? Which do I need to work on?
- Which items give me the highest payoff? Which of the items have a negative payoff?
- What will happen if I do not do this today?
- Of all the things I have to do, which will make me feel best to get rid of?

As you plan your day, remember that you can deal only with discretionary time. There are significant blocks of time over which you have little or no control: meetings with clients, project meetings, sales calls (at the client's convenience), travel time, and staff meetings. Because they are either regularly scheduled or scheduled at the behest or convenience of others, there is little you can do about them. They are events you cannot control.

Build your list on your available discretionary time. Don't schedule 100 percent. If you have only 2 hours free, don't schedule 5 hours of work or even exactly 2 hours of activities. Schedule only the things you think you can handle. Try to anticipate the things that can be anticipated, but leave time to deal with the events that are not expected. Something for which you haven't planned is bound to come up.

One way to leverage your time power is to use obligations to your advantage. If you have a meeting with a client to discuss a current project, use the occasion to explore additional projects the client might be considering. Or ask the client to explain his or her industry so you can develop a greater understanding of the market. If you have to attend an office staff party in your role as figurehead of the firm, take the opportunity to celebrate the individual or team accomplishments or reinforce the values of the firm.

Dealing With Procrastination

Procrastination is a major reason why people don't always do what they say they are going to do. It has a variety of causes, but they are less important than what you can do to avoid it. Here are some techniques and tips avoiding procrastination.

The *salami technique* consumes a project one small slice at a time. It takes an activity that seems to require a large block of uninterrupted time and breaks it into tasks that don't take much time to do. Not only does it make the project less daunting; it provides a wealth of short tasks that you can do in 10- and 15-minute openings in your schedule. (Those are the times when you look at your to-do list and see that although your top priority is working on a proposal, you don't have enough time right now, so you might as well do something easy—and usually less important.)

If the project is preparing a proposal, the steps might include reviewing the request for proposal, researching the prospect and his or her needs, contacting consultants, and preparing a budget. Each step is divided into smaller and smaller steps. Preparing the budget involves assembling historical information, assessing the scope of services, developing a labor schedule, and assigning costs. Each action is subdivided until you reach the smallest individual steps possible, such as identifying the files that have the necessary information, assembling those files, and making a list of phone numbers of people you must contact for information. You can do those things, which should be listed chronologically, whenever you have a few minutes of free time.

A variation of this approach (a subset of the hors d'oeurve approach), is the *swiss cheese method*. It is for people who aren't systematic enough to use the salami technique. It gets its name because, by taking action, you begin to poke holes in the project. Each action you take makes another hole until you get the project done.

Begin by doing something, anything, related to your priority. If you need to prepare a budget for a proposal, you might get out the files, develop a list of costs and expenses, or place a call to a consultant to get an estimate for the services. Taking action builds momentum, so that you continue doing other things relating to this project. Once past the initial obstacle—of beginning—it becomes easier to continue.

Some tasks don't easily break down into discrete units. For example, you may have a stack of papers to file or a report to write. If you have a hard time starting, make an appointment with yourself to spend 5 minutes at that activity. Your commitment is limited—only 5 minutes. After the time is up, ask yourself whether you want to continue another 5 minutes, and then another, and so on. You will find that the hardest part of doing something is beginning.

At the start of the day, you face a list of priority items. Which one should you start with? The *worst first school* says that it is better to start with the least-pleasant task. The reasoning is that things are more unpleasant in the anticipation than in the doing. Once you get through the most onerous activity, things are easier the rest of the day. When you have to make marketing calls, start out with the most difficult prospect. If the call is successful, you build confidence to continue. If the result is not positive, nothing can be worse than that call, so things will probably get better.

Other people do just the opposite. They begin with the easiest task to increase the chance of starting the day with a success. They get a sense of accomplishment at the outset and build momentum and confidence for the more rigorous tasks ahead. The approaches are equally valid. Use the one with which you are most comfortable.

When you begin work on your first priority, assemble all the relevant materials and put everything else away. Keep all lower priority materials—papers, magazines, files, mail—out of sight so you can concentrate on the matter at hand. Nonessential materials on your desk or within your field of vision only distract you from your priority activity. They remind you of other, less important things that you need or want to do.

One designer told of using this technique to reduce stress. He traveled a great deal, and whenever he returned to his office, the piles of paper on and around his desk grew higher and deeper. Working in his office surrounded by the swelling stacks, he felt anxious and uneasy. Finally, he cleaned house, throwing out most of the papers and putting those he wanted to read in a closet. Afterward, he no longer felt stressed. Safely out of sight, the papers were no longer a source of anxiety.

The Ivy Lee story is a staple of time management folklore that teaches a very important lesson. In 1930, Lee was consultant to Charles Schwab, then the president of Bethlehem Steel. One day, Schwab asked Lee to suggest ways in which he could use his time more effectively. Lee responded by telling Schwab to write down the most important things he had to do that day, in order of their importance. At the beginning of the day, Lee said, start on the most important activity and don't stop until it is completed. Once the number 1 task is finished, go on to number 2 and don't stop until that, too, is done. Then go to number 3, number 4, and so on.

At the end of the day, Lee said, you may not have finished all the items on your list, but you will at least know that you have taken care of the most important ones. Several weeks later, according to the story, Schwab sent Lee a check for $25,000 with a note saying it was the most important management lesson he had ever learned.

The lesson is simple: First things first. Start on the most important activity first and don't stop until you complete it or you can proceed no further. That may happen if, for example, you have to wait for someone else to give you information. Then move on to the second activity and don't stop until you have completed it. And so on.

Time Wasters

Time wasters keep you from working on your priorities. They can be either external or internal. External time wasters come from someone or something else; they are the result of the system or of other people's actions or attitudes. Internal time wasters are self-imposed; they are the result of your own attitudes and behaviors. Figure 8.1 lists some external and internal time wasters.

External

Employees with problems
Telephone
Lunch
Interruptions
Meetings
Poor communication
Routine work
Lack of competent personnel
Visitors
Junk mail
Negative attitudes
Waiting for feedback
Mistakes of others
Understaffing

Internal

Attempting too much at once
Unrealistic time estimates
Unclear or ambiguous goals and objectives
Lack of planning
Lack of organization
Unable to say no
Refusal to delegate or delegating responsibility without authority
Snap decisions
Blaming others
Bypassing the organization
Lack of clear priorities
Too involved in details.
Lack of self-discipline
Indecision

Figure 8.1. Typical time wasters.

Most time wasters seem to be external, the result of other people's actions and thus beyond your control. It is true that you cannot dictate other people's behavior, but you *can* control your response to the situation. In so doing, you influence the way others deal with you. The following discussion of interruptions shows how you can bring what seems to be an external time waster under your control.

Interruptions

Interruptions are inevitable, no matter how well you plan your time. Therefore, you need to develop strategies to deal with them. One strategy is to build extra time into estimates of how long it will take to do something. Allot 20 or 25 minutes for a task that will take 15 minutes of uninterrupted time. If you can get it done in 15 minutes, you are that much ahead.

A second approach is to anticipate interruptions and plan for them so they won't happen. For example, assume that one or two staff members interrupt you regularly. You can short-circuit their interruptions by scheduling regular meetings with them. They can collect questions and information items to review at those meetings, rather than always having to interrupt you.

Your time log will suggest how often these meetings should be. With some people, it might be only once a week; with others, it might be twice a day. Knowing he or she will have access to you within a reasonable time, the employee doesn't need to interrupt you; there are very few situations that can't wait an hour or two to be resolved.

Don't reward people for interrupting you. If someone disturbs you when you don't want to be bothered and you give him or her your attention, your actions say that it's OK to interrupt you. The way to get people to respect your requests not to be interrupted is to not deal with them when they do. Don't answer their questions or give them information. Instead, politely but firmly tell them that you can't be disturbed now and that you will talk to them later. And do talk to them later. If you are consistent in that, you will show them that you are serious about not being disturbed.

Calls from clients are a sensitive matter. Because you are in a service business, you want to be responsive. At the same time, you must control your time. If a client calls when you don't want to be interrupted, have your secretary take the message and tell your client you will call him or her back at a specific time, say 10:15 a.m. or 3:45 p.m. Most people don't mind being put off if they know when you will return the call.

What they object to is the message "He'll call you back." Not only is it vague; it obligates them to be indefinitely available.

The best time to plan for being uninterrupted is when you already have the fewest interruptions. A review of your time log will give you that information. One architect does his design work early in the morning, from 2:00 to 7:00 a.m., when he is free from phone calls and other people. An interior designer works at home from 6:00 to 10:00 a.m. before going to her office. Her office situation doesn't provide the kind of privacy she needs, so she finds it elsewhere.

Time-Saving Tips

Match activities to your energy level. As you go through the day, your energy level rises and falls. Some people function best in the morning, others in the afternoon, and still others in the late evening or early morning. You can determine your peak times by tracking your energy level at the same time you keep your time log. While you record your activities, rate your physical and mental energy levels with the following scale: 5, high; 4, medium high; 3, medium; 2, medium low; 1, low. To simplify your analysis, record your ratings of physical energy in one color and ratings of mental energy in another. After you have completed your log, look for patterns. Are there particular times when you consistently have a great deal of energy? Are there times when your energy is consistently low?

Once you have figured out your patterns, plan activities when their physical and mental requirements match your energy level. If you are a morning person, schedule tasks for which you need the maximum mental energy, such as design work, for the morning hours. Don't schedule work that requires a great deal of thought in the afternoon if your energy is low then. That might be a good time to do things that are not mentally taxing, such as paperwork and filing.

Cluster your activities.   When you have a series of similar tasks, do them in a batch. If you have several letters to answer or bills to review, set aside a time to do them all at once rather than spread them out over the entire day. Set up office hours so that visitors know there is a time when you are always available.

Set aside certain times for making phone calls. Make sure they are when others are likely to be available. If the person you are trying to reach is not in, leave a message with specific times when you can be reached. He or she will appreciate knowing when you are available, and you will be disturbed by fewer calls during the times when you need to concentrate. If you have difficulty getting through to someone, make a phone appointment: Arrange for a definite time when the person will be there to take your call.

Look through your second- and third-class mail only once a week. Since that type of mail is not time-sensitive, you don't need to look at it immediately. But it may be interesting to you, or it may have some informational value.

Handle a paper only once, to the extent that is possible. You don't have to take care of it immediately, but once you begin, take whatever action is necessary to get it to the next step: Prepare an answer, write a reply, file it, toss it, or give it to someone else for follow-up.

Use two easy techniques to save time spent in handling correspondence. To answer a letter requesting a small amount of specific information — a name, address, or approval on some item — don't write a new letter in reply. Just jot your answer in the margin or at the bottom of the letter. Copy the letter and return the original. Not only does that conserve your time; it is efficient for the writer because both the original request and your answer are on one piece of paper.

Another shortcut is to use two-way memos. Available from commercial printers, the two-page forms, with interleaved carbon-paper, have a memo at the top and space for a reply memo on the bottom. You write your request at the top and send the entire form. The addressee writes his or her reply on the bottom, sends you back the original and retains the copy for filing. The reply has both the request and the answer on the same page, which saves paper, time, and filing space.

Take time to think. It is all too easy to get caught up in doing something and lose sight of why you are doing it. You can prevent that by using the following technique. Prior to beginning an activity, remind yourself of what you want to accomplish. Before you call a client or consultant, ask yourself what your purpose is and what result you hope for. Do you want a specific piece of information, a decision, an approval of your decision, or do you just want to let the person know you are available? Asking yourself those questions allows you to focus on your priorities and not get sidetracked into irrelevant conversation.

When a visitor or staff member drops in unexpectedly, ask what he or she wants. That gives you the chance to decide whether his or her purpose is more important than what you are doing at the moment. If it is, you can deal with the person; if it is not, ask him or her to come back later.

Being aware of what you want to accomplish doesn't have to stifle spontaneity. There may be times when you decide to do something despite your priorities because it feels right. There is nothing wrong with that; intuition is sometimes a better guide to what is important than logic. There will be other times when you have to turn from your priorities because a situation that you hadn't anticipated arises.

The more you are aware of them, the more you can shape your actions to achieve your purposes. By monitoring your purposes and your priorities, you decide how to use your time based on a considered judgment of what is important to you.

Use blank time.   Make productive use of the time you spend commuting or driving to and from appointments. Use your car cassette recorder (or an ultraportable) to listen to books on tape or one of the large selection of taped management seminars and self-help programs. Carry a microcassette tape recorder to record your thoughts, ideas, questions, and notions about current and future projects. If you drive a great deal, consider getting a cellular phone so you can conduct business from your car.

Whenever you leave your office, take material related to a high-priority item with you. That way, if you get to an appointment early or find you have to wait, you always have something on which to work. Since you are effectively insulated from phone calls, such times are very useful for doing reading.

Working harder isn't working smarter. When you are doing something, be aware of the return you are getting from your effort. If you are productive and are making progress, it makes sense to continue. When you reach the point of diminishing returns, your productivity plummets and your energy is largely wasted. At that point, go on to something else.

Take a strategic break from intense concentration. When you are doing brain work, your mental efficiency drops dramatically after about an hour. Recharge your creative energy and restore your productivity by taking a 5- or 10-minute break to exercise or walk around.

Take care of yourself. One of the best ways to use your time effectively is to keep yourself in good health. Poor health drains both your energy and your effectiveness. Time invested in your own well-being has a high return. Exercise regularly to keep your energy up and your stress level down.

How to Make Meetings
Meaningful

Meetings are unavoidable. The collaborative nature of design requires the involvement of different people, all of whom participate in the process and must be involved to one extent or another. Much of this occurs in meetings. The following are some suggestions for making meetings more effective. They will save you time and make the time you spend in meetings more productive.

1. Be clear on the purposes of the meeting. Know what you want to accomplish and select a group process that is appropriate for those purposes. Many of these techniques are described in Chapter 7.

2. Most meetings are called to accomplish a task. If that task is to generate ideas, use a process that fosters individual participation and creativity and allows participants to play their ideas off one another. Techniques such as brainstorming and the nominal group method are useful for this purpose.

3. If the group will make a decision, such as giving its recommendations or choosing among alternatives, a different process is in order. If the decision is important and you have the time, consensus is the most effective method. Otherwise, have the members choose by majority vote.

4. Some meetings are used to persuade people to approve a course of action that you have formulated. In that situation, you need to control both the process and the content of the meeting. People are most likely to go along when they see that they can achieve their own ends through the group's activity. Your goal in this type of meeting is to get them to create such expectations. You can do that by having them articulate their needs and then demonstrate how those needs can be met through your proposal.

5. Some meetings are called for informational purposes. If you want to disseminate information, you need to control both the content and the process to ensure that there is clear communication and people understand what is being said. If the purpose is sharing information, you need to make sure that everyone has a chance to speak.

6. A second basic reason for meetings is to give participants the chance to relate to one another. Meetings give members of a project team a chance to size each other up and to get comfortable with working together; they give clients the chance to reaffirm their trust in your abilities as designer; and they give your staff members a chance to reaffirm with their colleagues that they share values and attitudes.

7. Monitor the meeting's progress to make sure there is an appropriate balance between the task and relationship functions. Meetings that are too oriented toward the social end tend to not get much accomplished. Those that are solely task-focused begin to be like a steamroller; they cause participants to feel that they have been manipulated.

8. Invite to a meeting only the people who need to be there. That keeps people who don't need to be there from wasting their time when they could be expending their efforts more profitably elsewhere.

9. Meetings often have more than one purpose. To guarantee that everyone knows what will happen and what is expected, prepare a written agenda before the meeting. That will help you determine what process to use for each item. Give participants the written agenda before the meeting and review agenda items before starting to conduct business. That prepares participants for the discussion.

10. Start meetings on time. When you don't start on time, the people who are prompt are penalized. Also, a prompt start trains participants to be on time; if the meeting is always held for them, it doesn't matter when they arrive. Your own behavior sets the standard. If you set a precedent by being on time, your staff will follow your lead.

11. Let participants know at the beginning of a meeting how long it will last. You can enforce meeting discipline by appointing someone to keep time throughout the meeting and notify the group when there is 30, 15, and 5 minutes left. If the meeting has to go over its allotted time, participants who have pressing business elsewhere should be able to leave without specific sanction.

12. During the last 5 minutes of a meeting, summarize what you have accomplished and what needs to be done as a result. This reinforces a sense of accomplishment, provides people with closure, and reminds them of the follow-up that needs to happen.

13. Publish a summary of what was said and accomplished in the meeting. This serves several purposes. It acts as a record of what happened to which participants can refer later. This can be useful if people leave the meeting unclear about the conclusions reached or if their correct understandings later become fuzzy. Summaries provide a paper trail that can avoid misunderstandings. People tend to forget what they have accomplished; they prefer to spotlight what they haven't done. As a record of what has been done, the summary reinforces a sense of accomplishment.

Delegation

One of the most effective ways to save time is to delegate work. When properly done, it enables you to leverage your time and knowledge. But for people who like doing, delegation can be very difficult. The following guidelines will help you increase your delegating power and personal productivity:[3]

1. *Make sure that your people are capable of doing the job.*   The first step in effective delegation is effective hiring. For you to be confident that someone can do a job, he or she must have the appropriate experience, abilities, and competence.

This guideline has two implications in practice. First, you need a clear idea of what you want a new person to do before you begin recruiting. Second, before you delegate a task to someone, you must feel confident that he or she can do it. If you don't, your attempt at delegation will be doomed at the outset. (Recruiting and hiring are discussed more fully in Chapter 5.)

2. *Spend time in training.*   Once you have identified the persons you want to take on a task, invest whatever time is necessary to train them. If your staff has the potential but not the experience to do the job, figure out a way to give them the experience.

3. *Clearly define what you expect of your staff members and confirm that they understand it.*   This is the most crucial part of delegation, and it is also the most poorly done. It is your responsibility to make sure that the person knows exactly what you want. In the vast majority of instances, when an individual fails to carry out an assigned task, the failure can be traced to poor instructions and supervision.

Here is a simple way to check on whether someone understands your instructions. Ask him to tell you in his own words his interpretation of the assignment. His summary of your charge will show whether you have been successful in your communication.

4. *Let employees know how much initiative they can take.*   Delegation can involve many levels of responsibility. You can ask someone to do something exactly as you say, without any changes at all. You can ask a staff member to research a situation and develop a set of options. You can ask him or her to recommend one alternative from several possibilities, and then go do it. Or you can ask the person to research a situation, implement the most appropriate course, and report the results to you.

Be sure the employee understands how much autonomy he or she has to act. Make sure the person knows when and how you will review and approve his or her work. The clearer you are on each of these points, the better the employee will know the rules of the game and be able to operate within them.

---

[3] See Alan C. Filley, *The Compleat Manager*, Green Briar Press, Middleton, Wisconsin, pp. 135–138, 1978.

5. *Get the employee's commitment.*   Giving an assignment is only half the work of delegation; gaining a commitment is the other part. If an employee makes a specific commitment to something, the employee is more likely to follow through and do a good job on it than if he or she was ordered to do it. Obtaining that commitment forms a contract: it binds the employee to the task by his or her word.

6. *Don't do their work for them.*   It is often difficult for a principal to let people do their own work. That is especially true if someone is not doing a good job. The employee comes to you saying that he or she is stuck, that he or she can't make a decision, or that he or she can't come up with a solution. The person throws the task back to you. If you are action-oriented like most principals, you will sigh and do the work yourself. All the time, however, you will be frustrated because no one can do it as well as you can.

It may, of course, be true that the employee can't do it as well as you can, but if you take the job back, you have defeated your purpose. By doing the work yourself, you show the employee that he or she won't be held accountable for his or her performance. The point of delegation is to have the employee do the work, not you. A more appropriate response is to tell the person to complete the assignment. He or she is being paid to do that work and should be held accountable. When the employee is done, review the work and make suggestions and comments. If the employee doesn't complete the assignment, to which he or she is committed, the employee should take the consequences.

7. *Reward employees for taking initiative.*   If the employee takes initiative and does a good job, reward him or her. The rewards can be either monetary and non-monetary. Whichever you use, the work should be noted and celebrated. (See Chapter 5 for a discussion of rewards.)

Summary

This chapter has presented a number of suggestions for increasing your personal effectiveness:

- Take time to plan your day.
- Set priorities for your daily activities.
- Don't schedule yourself 100 percent; allow time for unanticipated occurrences.
- Use the salami technique: cut projects into small slices.
- Use the swiss cheese method: poke holes in projects by taking some kind of action.

- Make a 5-minute appointment with yourself.
- Do the worst task first...or the easiest.
- Focus only on your priority project.
- Start on your top-priority project and don't stop until you complete it.
- Anticipate and plan for interruptions.
- Don't reward people for interrupting you.
- Plan uninterrupted time when experience shows you usually have the least interruptions.
- Match activities with your energy level.
- Cluster activities.
- Take time to think and center yourself.
- Keep in good health.
- Always be aware of what your priorities are.
- Fill in blank time.

Recommended Reading

Allen, Jane Elizabeth, *Beyond Time Management*, Addison-Wesley, Reading, Massachusetts, 1986.

Bliss, Edwin C., *Doing It Now*, Bantam, New York, 1983.

Ellis, Albert and William J. Knaus, *Overcoming Procrastination*, New American Library, New York, 1977.

Filley, Alan C., *The Compleat Manager*, Green Briar Press, Middleton, Wisconsin, 1978.

Kriegel, Robert J. and Marilyn Harris Kriegel, *The C Zone*, Ballantine, New York, 1984.

Lakein, Alan, *How to Get Control of Your Time and Your Life*, New American Library, New York, 1973.

Mackenzie, R. Alec, *The Time Trap*, AMACOM, New York, 1972.

Schlenger, Sunny and Roberta Roesch, *How to Be Organized in Spite of Yourself*, New American Library, New York, 1989.

9

Changing the Practice

The successful practice learns from its experience. By learning not to repeat the same mistakes, it can do what it does best. By learning to learn, it can improve the way it does what it does.

Learning requires specific effort. Without it, the lessons from a practice's history and memory promote stagnation over adaptation, rigidity over responsiveness. Even when a practice is small, learning can be stifled and flexibility inhibited by organizational structures, systems, and behavior. The first part of this chapter discusses how an organization learns—and doesn't learn.

Learning leads to change. Change is constant: Innovations in technology and design concepts appear with increasing frequency. Projects become more complex: Clients grow more sophisticated every day in their understanding of design and their demands on designers. Solutions that worked last week become outmoded in 6 months; ideas that weren't appropriate last month may be just right next year.

Every shift in circumstances, every new idea, and every improvement requires a corresponding adjustment. To cope with such dynamic conditions, the practice has to be flexible. Your practice is a series of adaptations to change. People respond to change in different ways. Some people welcome it; some resent it; others are indifferent. Figure 9.1 lists some reasons why people welcome or resist change.

Managing change requires several critical skills; they include knowing how people will respond to change, helping people to overcome their

Figure 9.1. Why people resist or welcome change. (*Donald Kirkpatrick,* **How to Manage Change Effectively,** *pp. 85–88.*

Reasons for Resisting Change

The individual may lose:
   Security
   Money
   Pride and satisfaction
   Friends and important contacts
   Freedom
   Responsibility
   Authority
   Good working conditions
   Status or prestige

The individual has or sees no need for the change.

The change will do more harm than good for the individual.

The individual lacks respect for the person making the change.

The change is announced or made in an objectionable manner.

The individual has a negative attitude.

The individual has no input into the decision for change.

The change is seen as a personal criticism.

The change creates burdens for the individual.

The change requires effort.

The timing is bad.

The change is seen as a challenge to authority.

The individual hears about the change through second-hand information.

Reasons for Accepting Change

The individual may gain:
   Security
   Money
   Authority
   Status or prestige

(*Continued*)

Figure 9.1. (*Continued*)

Responsibility

Better working conditions

Self-satisfaction

Better personal contacts

Less time and effort

The change will provide new challenges.

The individual likes or respects the source of the change.

The individual likes the manner in which the change is made.

The change will reduce the individual's boredom.

The individual has input into the decision on change.

The individual desires change.

The change will improve the individual's future.

The timing is good.

---

resistance, and increase their commitment, and being able to make the change stick. The remainder of the chapter describes a model for making changes followed by a case study of one firm's experience.

Organizational Learning

Levels of Learning

Organizational learning occurs at many levels.[1] The most basic learning takes place when an error is fixed. That is what happens when you get a change order on a project because of an error or omission. The change order is an indication of a problem in the construction documents. The usual response is to make the necessary changes and proceed.

The next level occurs when you take steps to prevent the problem from occurring. Typically, that is done by increasing the monitoring of the production process. A practice will initiate a quality assurance procedure in which documents are reviewed before they are submitted. The more frequent the reviews, the more quickly problems can be picked up and corrected.

---

[1] The notion of levels of learning is based upon Harold Sirkin and George Stalk, Jr., "Fix the Process, Not the Problem," *Harvard Business Review*, pp. 26–33, July–August 1990.

A third level of learning occurs when you look for root causes of a problem. That requires a more sophisticated inquiry. In the case of production problems, you may analyze the number and type of change orders from several projects over a period of time. Your analysis might reveal patterns that point to underlying causes, and your solutions would then focus on changing the process to eliminate the problems.

One firm found that many of its production problems could be traced to inadequate design development: Pressures to turn out work and bill clients led them to a short-circuiting of that phase of the process. As a result, problems that should have been worked out in design development either were never addressed or were slipping through. When the process was changed to provide adequate design development, the error rate—and the subsequent expense of making changes—dropped considerably.

The highest level of learning is the anticipatory level. At that level, you develop solutions to problems that haven't yet occurred. An example of this type of learning is found at The Axton Group, a small architectural firm whose production process is highly computerized. Consultants working with the firm use compatible equipment linked to the practice. When one of the consultants or the designer makes a change, it is immediately transmitted to all the other members of the team and integrated into their plans. The improved coordination cuts down the number of errors that are due to poor communication among team members.

Another example of anticipatory learning is a technique developed by Perkins & Will to resolve the dilemma of balancing project costs with program requirements. This is a prime source of problems that can lead to cost overruns, conflict between designer and architect, and major changes after work on the project has begun. To avoid such problems, Perkins and Will conducts a predesign exercise with the client to explore the tradeoff between cost, quality, and program. Examining these issues at the beginning of the project gives both client and designer an opportunity to resolve conflicts at the outset rather than later, when changes will be costly and contentious.

Single- and Double-Loop Learning

A practice learns to do things better by using single-loop learning.[2] The learning sequence begins when the practice establishes standards of

---

[2] The concepts of single- and double-loop learning are discussed at length in Chris Argyris and Donald Schon, *Organizational Learning: A Theory of Action Perspective,* Addison-Wesley, Reading, Massachusetts, 1978.

performance. It then monitors its performance to compare what it is doing with those standards. When the performance diverges from the standards, corrective action is taken.

Project budgeting is an example of single-loop learning. When you create a budget, you set standards of performance for the project team: how many hours and dollars should spent on each phase of the project. You monitor performance by analyzing time sheets and project financial reports. When you see a discrepancy between the budget and performance—when you find that one phase is substantially over or under budget—you get the project manager to do something about it.

Double-loop learning takes the inquiry beyond performance; it also tests the appropriateness of the criteria. If the standards are found to be inadequate or inappropriate, they are changed. When you engage in double-loop learning, you analyze the budget process itself as well as how well you do in meeting the budget. If experience shows that you are consistently over budget in the production phase, no matter what the type of project, double-loop learning suggests that you need to examine how you formulate the budget. You may need to change your guidelines to get a more realistic budget in the first place.

Single-loop learning is concerned solely with performance. The first two learning levels described above, fixing errors and preventing errors, are examples of this type of learning. Double-loop learning probes both performance and process. It includes the two higher levels of learning described above: the search for root causes and anticipatory learning.

For a practice to reach its full potential, it should engage in both single- and double-loop learning. The problem, however, is that the conditions that make it possible to be effective in single-loop learning may inhibit or prevent double-loop learning.

People in a practice usually have only a partial understanding of and interest in what the organization is doing. Everyone has his or her own picture of the situation, and that picture is necessarily incomplete. Designers are interested mainly in design; production people are concerned only with production; and support staff usually don't know much about projects. This fragmentation of viewpoint is often reinforced by structure and hierarchy. People at lower levels have a much more constricted view of the practice than those at higher levels.

When information doesn't flow freely from the principals to employees or from one part of the practice to another, these partial images are strengthened. The result is that people pursue their own goals; they are unaware or unconcerned with how they fit into the total picture. This fragmentation creates political and psychological barriers to double-loop learning.

Furthermore, employees are usually expected to be concerned solely with their own responsibilities and not with other parts of the practice. The reward system reinforces that view. Most compensation programs reward employees for individual performance rather than for performance of the team or the practice as a whole.

In many practices, there are unspoken norms against challenging the status quo. Staff members are expected to perform, not question the way projects are scheduled or budgeted. But that is exactly what is required in double-loop learning.

Another factor that inhibits double-loop learning is the notion of accountability. When people are held accountable for their performances, they are rewarded for success and punished (or at least not rewarded) for failure. But in a system that punishes failure, people have an incentive to protect themselves when they don't meet expectations. They may tell you what they think you want to hear, or they may manage impressions to make themselves look better. They can go to great lengths to soften the impact of bad news, or they can try to avoid responsibility and deflect blame.

A third inhibiting factor comes from the differences that usually exist between what a practice says and what it does. If actions are not congruent with the stated goals or policies of the practice, people may try to gloss over the gap. They may engage in rationalizations, rhetoric, or diversionary behavior to cover that fact.

These factors stimulate behavior that conceals or disguises the true situation, which makes it difficult to confront problems and deal with the realities of the situation. In your behavior and your attitudes, you can act to offset those inhibiting factors. Accept the inevitability of uncertainty. Since surprises will always happen, see them as challenges. Accept problems as opportunities to learn. Adopt an open and reflective attitude toward error.

When analyzing and solving problems, search for as many viewpoints as possible. Avoid imposing arbitrary structures on situations. Be open to different ways to define and redefine problems. Embrace diversity and competing viewpoints as a means of fully exploring the issues. Let solutions emerge through consensus rather than impose them by an exercise of power. Let action be driven by inquiry, not by formula. Question the status quo. Always probe for improvements and innovation.

Those conditions for fostering double-loop learning should be familiar to you. They are the same as those that stimulate creativity in the design process. At its highest level, the design process is an example of double-loop learning.

Changing the Practice

A Model for Initiating Changes

There are effective and ineffective ways to make changes. Since change is inevitable, it makes sense to manage it properly so you can get the greatest benefits from your efforts. You can introduce change in your practice systematically.[3] There are seven steps in the process:

1. Determine the need for change

2. Prepare a tentative plan

3. Analyze possible reactions

4. Make a final decision

5. Establish a timetable

6. Communicate the change

7. Implement the change

Following a discussion of each step, the process is illustrated by the following case study of GGR, an architectural practice, in which a new principal tries to get the firm to use CAD.

1. *Determine the need for change.* First, you have to recognize that a problem exists. The change process begins with your awareness that things aren't working as well as they should or that you can do better. This recognition can come from many sources. Shifts in the economy, market conditions, or client needs and expectations can cause you to reassess the way you are doing things. Technological advances may affect the way you handle projects and do design.

Another stimulus for change is pain. Eroding profits, chronically poor performance, ineffective scheduling, employee complaints, and turnover are painful symptoms that cry out for attention.

Finally, the desire for excellence is a strong force for change; it encourages a constant search for innovation and improvement.

Once the problem is acknowledged, you have to decide what changes are needed. Here you must consider the other people in the practice. As much as is possible, involve them in the decision making that is necessary to identify and effect the changes. This has several benefits. People who participate in decision making are more likely to be committed to

---

[3] The process for managing change is discussed in more detail in Donald L. Kirkpatrick, *How to Manage Change Effectively*, Jossey-Bass, San Francisco, California, pp. 85–88, 1985.

the change and less likely to resist change. With less resistance, the solution can be implemented more quickly. Participation promotes the exploration of different viewpoints that is helpful to double-loop learning. This increases the chances that you will come up with a higher quality solution to the problem that prompted the changes.

Different situations call for different levels of participation. The Vroom-Yetton decision model discussed in Chapter 7 is a useful guideline for determining appropriate levels of involvement in decision making.

2. *Prepare a tentative plan.* Once you have determined that a change is necessary, the next step is to develop a tentative plan. The plan needs to be provisional at this point so you can test it on the people who will be affected. Their responses may cause you to modify it in order to increase acceptance and reduce resistance.

When you discuss the plan with others, it is important to make the others feel their ideas are gaining a fair hearing. If they get the impression that you are not listening, they will become resentful. That may lead them to be less open and honest in giving their opinions about the changes and it may also cause them to resist the changes.

Planning for change is similar to strategic planning as described in Chapter 2. The major difference is that a plan for change concentrates on a specific problem area, whereas a strategic plan looks at the practice as a whole.

The plan must be as specific as possible about what the practice will look like after the changes. The more details you can provide, the more real the plan becomes—both to you and to others. Such a description reinforces the positive aspects of the future; it pulls people's attention away from the effort involved in the change. Like your vision for the practice, it becomes a magnet attracting people to it instead of pushing people away from the present.

A detailed description also helps those who are not involved in the decision process to understand what you want and how they fit in. If they don't have such information, they will draw their own conclusions, which will probably be negative and will lead to resentment and resistance.

Besides describing what the practice will look like when the change is fully implemented, you must also describe the transitional stages. Work backward from your desired end state to two or three interim steps. Describe each of the stages in as much detail as the end state. This will help your staff understand not only where you want to go but also how you intend to get there.

3. *Analyze possible reactions.* People react to change in many ways. Some accept it or welcome it; others resent it or actively resist it; still

others are indifferent or have mixed reactions (Figure 9.1). In order to change your practice, you first have to change the behavior of the people within it. People respond to change with both their heads and their hearts. Their responses will determine how effective the change will be. Thus, you need to understand the feelings of those who will be affected so you can act to shape those responses.

Two factors shape an individual's response to change: commitment and capability. A person is committed to change to the extent that he or she is willing, motivated, and oriented toward the goals of the change. A person is capable of change to the extent that he or she has the power, authority, and influence to allocate resources to the change as well as the information and the skills to carry it out.

In assessing people's responses, you need to identify (1) the key people in the change effort, (2) how they will react, and (3) how to increase their acceptance (or neutralize their resistance) to the minimum level necessary to implement the change. Draw up a list of people who will be most affected by the change. Indicate those who are necessary to make the change work. Rate them first on their readiness and their capability to make the change: Is their readiness high, medium, or low? Then rate their general commitment to the change: Will they resist it? Will they be neutral? Will they let it happen? Will they help it happen? Will they make it happen? Finally, note any ideas you have about what you need to do to change their attitudes or capabilities.

That will give you the information necessary to devise strategies to get people to be willing to change, which will be when the benefits of change outweigh the costs of changing. An individual's willingness is the product of three elements: the level of dissatisfaction with the status quo, the desirability of the proposed change or result, and the practicality of the proposed change for the individual, the level of risk, and the disruption the change entails. When the product of those factors is greater than the cost, the individual will be willing to change. In devising your strategy, you can work on any of the three factors for each person or group involved in the change.

4. *Make a final decision.* Having discussed the tentative plan and received input and feedback, you must now come up with a final plan. One consideration is how you will make the decision on the plan. Again the issue is the degree of participation: will you decide yourself or will you involve others? The Vroom-Yetton model described in Chapter 7 can be helpful in this determination.

5. *Establish a timetable.* Change takes time, and the amount of time will vary with the circumstances. If people are highly committed, you can move more quickly than if you expect resistance. Conversely, the

more resistance there is, the more difficult it will be to make the change and the longer the change will take to make.

Changes that are imposed take less time to decide and initiate but longer to integrate into normal organizational behavior. Coerced changes are more likely to lead to resistance, which complicates implementation. Changes that are the result of a participative process take longer to decide but can be implemented in a shorter period. Also, the change will last longer. That is because participation builds commitment.

6. *Communicate the change.*   Communication is critical to successful implementation. Change, positive or negative, causes anxiety and stress; communication helps to reduce these effects. Let people know in advance why you are making the changes. The more they understand and accept the reasons for change, the less anxious they will be and the less they will resist.

You are better off giving people too much information rather than too little. It is also better to let more people than necessary know of the impending change than to keep some people in the dark.

7. *Implement the change.*   You can initiate change in many ways. You can impose it whether or not people are willing participants, or you can let it emerge from the collective participation of yourself and your employees. There is no one best way to implement change. You need a strategy that is appropriate to the specific situation.

The first question of implementation is where to start. Change can begin in many places. You can start it from the top, in which case you and the other principals (if there are any) model the new behavior. If communicated effectively, this can be a very powerful approach: It was used by the principal of a medium-sized architecture and interior design firm who wanted his staff members to be more effective in their use of time. He began using a daily planner in a very visible way. His behavior became a model for project managers, who then began to use the same system.

Another place to begin is with people or groups who are ready and eager for change. Because of their interest and commitment, you can make the changes quickly. An early success makes a convincing case to others that the changes are worthwhile. That was how the principal at GGR initiated the use of CAD in his office. (See the case study below.)

You can begin where the pain is greatest. When pain begins to inhibit effective functioning, it becomes a forceful motivating factor for change. When the principals of a medium-size architectural and interior design firm in California assessed the firm's situation, they concluded that the most immediate problem was cash flow. Though they had sufficient work, the poor flow of cash threatened to strangle their operation. They realized that they needed to change quickly or risk losing the firm.

Another way is to create new teams or systems to implement the change. These new entities have no history, so they can function free from conventional wisdom. The California office of a major national architectural and engineering firm used this approach to stimulate design excellence. The firm brought in a new design principal to organize a skunk works whose charge was to do outstanding design. This team worked outside the existing framework, so it could set new standards of excellence and create innovative approaches to design.

A variation of this approach is to create temporary systems or projects. They might be teams or task forces to investigate or implement certain areas of change. Gensler and Associates used this strategy in a recent long-range planning effort. They formed 12 different task forces to address issues that affect both the quality of their design work and the completeness of the services they provide. Each task force identified immediate and long-range objectives and made recommendations on methods to accomplish those goals.

Initiating the Change

After figuring out where to start, you must determine how to initiate the change. Again, there is no one best approach. If the culture and traditions of the practice stifle change, you must take some action that will unfreeze the old ways. You may need to shock the system to get people away from their old ways and be receptive to new approaches. Organization-wide confrontation meetings and third-party interventions can help people understand how the culture inhibits learning and prevents change.

A large architectural-engineering firm conducted a two-day staff retreat to identify organizational issues and begin to develop solutions. The staff members first came up with seven priority issues. They then broke out into small groups to brainstorm ideas for ways to deal with each issue. The retreat focused attention on priorities, generated commitment, developed possible solutions, and provided the initial impetus for change. The firm followed up by creating committees to continue work in each of those areas.

If various people or parts of the practice don't share the same goals or priorities, you can conduct goal-setting exercises to build consensus. A medium-size architecture and interior design firm that resulted from a merger of two smaller firms held such a meeting soon after the merger. The meeting enabled the newly united principals and staff to become aware of their common values and begin to create a new organization.

Educational activities and learning situations give people new information, technical knowledge, and skills to make changes. ISD Interiors, a national interior design firm, uses such an approach to introduce CAD. Teams receive intensive training just before they begin a new project. They use the new project as a case study for applying the new techniques. By immediately applying the learning to their next project, the team quickly integrates the new behavior into its operations.

If the organizational design is inappropriate for the new situation, you may need to redesign all or part of the practice. A major change might involve a switch from one type of structure to another (see Chapter 4). A less-sweeping modification may require only the restructuring of one or more job descriptions.

A 70-person architectural firm in Southern California used this approach when faced with an ownership transition. For most of its life, it was configured as an innovative organization with the founder, who was also the chief designer, at the apex. Several years ago, the founder began grooming several people as a new generation of leaders. He created positions of associates and restructured the management of the firm to include their participation. He shifted the configuration from innovative to professional to accommodate the new reality.

If the change is significant, you should modify the reward system to reinforce the new behaviors. When Welton Becket merged with Ellerbe Inc. to form Ellerbe Becket, a new compensation program was created for top people in each office. Incentives were tied to the performance both of the individual office and the firm as a whole. This was meant as a visible reminder of the need for cooperation in order to make the merger work.

You can undertake changes on a small scale through pilot projects, which allow you to test approaches and modify them in a limited way before committing to a major effort. This is how GGR introduced CAD in it office. (See the following case study.)

Another way to try changes on a small scale is to set up experiments, which differ from pilot projects in that there is no commitment to implementation. If it works and the results are promising, an experiment can be extended to other parts of the practice. If it doesn't work, you go on to something else. Practices that engage in experimentation get a constant stream of new ideas without major expenditures of time and energy.

You can also impose change. That is often necessary when external circumstances call for a quick or harsh response. Forced change allows you to move more rapidly than if you involve people in the process.

Such a course is risky, however. When people are forced to do something, they have no commitment to it. The imposition of change may stimulate resentment or resistance. Those factors make it more difficult to implement the change.

Case Study: GGR Architects

In 1965, the founding principal of GGR (not its real name), a progressive 15-person architectural firm decided to introduce the latest in office technology. Bill spent thousands of dollars on typewriters and mag card machines. The equipment was delivered to the office without notice or fanfare. Though the staff was told about it, there was no orientation to or training on the machines. The boxes sat, unopened, for months and months. Finally, Bill became disgusted with the situation and hauled the machines away to storage.

In 1987, a new principal, Dan, suggested to his partners that they introduce CAD. He felt the change was needed for several reasons. It was the wave of the future and, besides, competitive firms were beginning to use it. GGR needed to keep up. He also felt that CAD would improve productivity and reduce errors.

Bill adamantly opposed the change. He had tried to introduce new technology before, but it didn't work. He felt that the staff was neither interested nor motivated enough to make new technology work. It would be a waste of money, just as it had been 20 years before.

Dan realized that unless he could change Bill's mind, there was no chance for CAD in the office. In 1989, Bill finally relented. Though he was still not persuaded that it would work, he agreed to let Dan set up a pilot project. Dan would have the opportunity to prove his case, and the firm would have to make only a limited investment.

After conducting extensive research, Dan developed specifications for the office's CAD system. The principals agreed on a budget for the initial equipment. Once he received approval from his partners, Dan thought about how he would involve the staff. He decided to tap the enthusiasm of two employees who had a particular interest in and knowledge of computers. After discussing the project with them, he authorized them to contact vendors and negotiate a contract for hardware and software based on the specifications and the budget.

The first benefit of this approach was that the two employees were able to get a better deal than Dan had thought possible. The original budget was supposed to be just enough to get a the basic hardware and software. Actually, the employees were able to get that system plus additional hardware and software.

Dan next considered how he would get the staff to use the system. He thought that Joe would be a good person to introduce CAD into the office. Joe was interested in computers; more important, his job was very repetitive: the design of relocatable classrooms. Joe was bored and wanted to do more meaningful work.

Dan made an arrangement with Joe. Joe would get training on the system, and he would then develop a way to put his current work on the computer. Once that happened, he could have another assignment; he would be freed to do "real architecture." Joe's other obligation would be to hold lunch-time seminars to train other staff to use the system.

Joe happily agreed and began his training. The new equipment is now in place, and people in GGR are beginning to use it.

Recommended Reading

Argyris, Chris, *Organizational Defenses*, Allyn & Bacon, Boston, 1990.

Argyris, Chris and Donald Schon, *Organizational Learning: A Theory of Action Perspective*, Addison-Wesley, Reading, Massachusetts, 1978.

Egan, Gerard, *Change-Agent Skills B: Managing Innovation and Change*, University Associates, San Diego, California, 1988.

Kirkpatrick, Donald L., *How to Manage Change Effectively*, Jossey-Bass, San Francisco, California, 1985.

Schon, Donald A., *The Reflective Practicioner*, Basic Books, New York, 1983.

Sirkin, Harold and George Stalk, Jr., "Fix the Process, Not the Problem," *Harvard Business Review*, pp. 26–33, July–August 1990.

Appendix A
Planning Worksheets

Worksheet 1: Mission Statement

A mission statement describes the basic thrust of your practice: what you do to earn your living. It should be short — three or four short sentences are sufficient — and explicit. It should be clear enough to let you know when you have succeeded.

Imagine that 5 years into the future, you have achieved all you set out to do 5 years before. Describe what you have accomplished. Ask yourself these questions: What types of work does your firm do? What kinds of services do you provide? What kinds of clients and projects do you have? Where does your firm do its work? How will you know whether or not you are successful?

Write your mission statement here:

Worksheet 2: Critical Success Factors

What must you accomplish to achieve your mission? What does it take to do *well* in this business? *Hint*: Think of others who in your opinion do very well at what you are trying to do and ask: What are they doing differently? For example, their contacts with referral sources may be superior, enabling them to get clients more easily. One CSF would then be *superior contacts with referral sources*. It could also be design excellence, location, a particular specialization, experience, better media exposure leading to greater reputation, and/or recognition.

A CSF is not the *how* of your practice; it is not directly manageable. Each CSF should be devoted to a single issue—do not use the word "and" in the statement. The list should be a mix of strategic and tactical factors. The maximum number of CSFs is eight.

The list of CSFs should meet the necessary-and-sufficient rule. Each CSF listed should be *necessary* to the mission; together, they should be *sufficient* to achieve the mission.

1.

2.

3.

4.

5.

6.

7.

8.

Worksheet 3: Assessing the Organization Against Critical Success Factors

Below, list each CSF and rate your organization against that factor on the following scale:

A = excellent performance

B = good performance

C = fair performance

D = poor performance

E = informal or embryonic performance or not being performed at all

Use the Comments column to explain your rating (For example, against what standard or other firm are you comparing yours?)

C S F	Score	Comments

Worksheet 4: Conducting a Cursory Environmental Scan

In each category below, list the assumptions you are making about trends that might affect how you do business, either positively or negatively.

1. Societal trends:

2. Demographic trends:

3. Economic trends:

4. Political trends:

5. Trends in technology:

6. Competitive trends:

7. Regulatory and legislative trends:

Worksheet 5: Defining Your Markets

1. Which services do you currently offer? Which would you like to offer?

2. How might you segment your clients? Typical ways include: type of work or project (residential, commercial, hospitality, etc.); location; client type (end user, corporate, governmental, developer, etc.); and budget (high-end, midlevel, etc.) Another way might be by sophistication of client about the design process. What other ways can you think of?

Think of each service you either currently offer or you would like to offer and answer the following questions. Use a separate sheet.

3. For *each* possible way to define your clients (see 2 above), ask the following:
   a. Does this method help me understand the needs of my clients?
   b. Does this method help me better satisfy client needs? If it does, why does it? How does it?

4. Which method is most helpful in understanding my clients?

5. Select the most promising way(s) to define your clients. Write out the segments each method gives you so you can compare them. Answer each of the following questions for each segment.
   a. Is this a segment I want to pursue?
   b. How will this segment grow in 1 to 5 years?
   c. How satisfied is this segment with you: __High __Medium __Low __NA

6. For each targeted segment, list the client's needs. Consider the following areas: types of services; price of services; quality of services; accessibility of services; your qualifications.

7. Rate your ability to meet each need:

   S = Superior

   G = Good

   F = Fair

   P = Poor

8. For each targeted segment, answer the following: Will this segment's needs change significantly in the next 3 to 5 years? How? Why? What impact will these changes have?

Worksheet 6: Identification of Competitors

1. Who else is in this business? (Who else does what you do and does it where you do it?)

2. What substitutes compete with you? (*Suggestion*: Look at your practice from the viewpoint of the client: To whom else can I turn for the same or similar service?)

3. For each *significant* competitor, complete the following questions:
   a. Who are its clients?

   b. How many clients does it currently serve?

   c. Is it planning to increase its client base or change its market targets?

   d. What services does it provide?

   e. Does it anticipate any significant changes in services in the future?

   f. What is its fee structure?

Worksheet 7: Determining Competitive Advantages

First identify all the differences between you and your competitors: differences in training, knowledge, and experience, in services provided — any differences you can think of. Then evaluate whether these differences are potential advantages or disadvantages. Finally, decide whether those advantages or disadvantages are substantial. They are if they are valued by clients and if your competitors can't easily eliminate the advantages or neutralize them.

1. For each *major* competitor, complete the following questions:
   a. What strengths that you have provide a difference between you and this competitor?

   b. Are the differences major or minor?

2. For each *major* difference:
   a. What is the size or extent of the difference?

   b. How do clients perceive the difference? Do they perceive it to be valuable?

   c. How have competitors responded to the difference?

   d. Is the difference a true competitive advantage?

3. Which strengths can become your most important competitive advantages?

4. Answer the following questions for the strengths identified in question 3.
   a. How well are you currently taking advantage of this strength?

   b. How can you take advantage of this strength in the future?

Worksheet 8: Identifying Opportunities

Given your mission (Worksheet 1), your competitive advantages (Worksheet 7), and the environmental trends you have identified (Worksheet 4), what future opportunities that you can identify should you consider? They can include: (1) continuing to do what you are presently doing, because an *unserved* or *underserved* demand for the service(s) or product(s) you provide still exists, (2) providing the same services to a larger market (clientele), (3) providing your present clientele with improved or new services or products, or (4) some combination of (2) and (3)—a new service for a new clientele.

Worksheet 9: Identifying Threats

What *external* trends or events could conceivably hinder or even curtail what you are currently trying to do? (You could be harmed by a potential competitor, a downturn in the economy, a regulation or legislation, an increase in costs, or a shortage of people with critical skills.) List the trends in a numbered fashion below the diagram. On the diagram place circled numbers corresponding to the threats you've listed where you think the threats lie in terms of impact and time frame. Naturally, you will be guessing now, but this exercise will tell you that you need to gather more concrete information later.

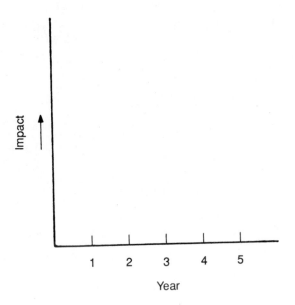

Worksheet 10: Goal Planning Sheet

1. Goal (specific, measurable, attainable, realistic, timely):

2. Benefits from achieving this goal:

3. Forces resisting attainment of this goal:

4. Forces assisting attainment of this goal:

5. What steps will you take to attain this goal?

6. How will you measure whether the goal has been reached?

Appendix B

Alternative Planning Techniques

Accelerated Planning Method

The *accelerated planning method* (APM)[1] is an intensive approach to planning; it provides a way to identify goals and the activities critical to their attainment and measure success. It is particularly useful when two or more people do the planning, because it ensures that everyone knows where the practice is headed, what is necessary to succeed, what must be done, and who is responsible for doing it. It is also a worthwhile method for sole practitioners or principals who have a small office without other managers.

The key participants in APM are the principals, but you should include anyone who is part of the management team. That might be the business manager, financial officer, or executive director; director of architecture or operations director; department or studio director; or associates who have management responsibilities. To keep the process effective and encourage individual participation, the group should have no more than 12 participants.

When a group is involved, APM is a collective process. Decisions are made by consensus. There is no voting, selling, or commanding. If you decide to use this process, you have to be prepared to accept the decisions of the group.

APM is conducted in an intensive 1- or 2-day session. All members of the management team should be there. If someone cannot be present, it is better to reschedule than to do it without that person. To get the max-

[1] The accelerated planning method is adapted from Maurice Hardaker and Bryan K. Ward, "How to Make a Team Work," *Harvard Business Review*, pp. 78–88, November–December 1984.

177

imum participation from those involved, the process should be facili- tated by a neutral party. The meetings should be held off premises, away from phones, secretaries, or any of the myriad distractions that are present at the office.

The first step is to get a clear idea of the shared sense of the practice's mission — what it is all about and what you want to accomplish. That is absolutely crucial, but it is not as easy as it may look. Too often, each of the principals in a practice has his or her individual ideas of what the mission is, but there is no shared vision. That is especially true of prac- tices that have formed out of a merger of two smaller offices. APM gets the participants to confront the issue of a shared vision.

The mission statement should be straightforward and concrete. It should be short — three or four sentences will suffice. It should clearly describe the services you provide, for whom you provide those services, where you provide the services, and how you will know whether you are achieving your mission.

Morris/Deasy/Dilday is a 20-person firm that used this method to de- velop its mission and plan. The three partners formulated the following mission:

> Morris/Deasy/Dilday provides a full range of architectural, space planning, and interior design services for a wide variety of project types to corporate and institutional clients in southern California, Arizona, and Nevada. We offer value to our clients through client and user satisfaction, excellence of design, innovation, recognition by the public and peers for design and leadership in the profession, and the pride and satisfaction of our principals and staff.

The next step is for the group to identify its critical success factors, the things it must do to accomplish its mission. Before doing that, how- ever, it is a good idea to get the group to loosen up its thinking. Take a 15-minute brainstorm break to come up with one-word descriptions of factors that might affect attainment of the mission. The rules for brain- storming are the following:

- Everyone should contribute.

- Everything is fair game, no matter how crazy or outrageous.

- No one is permitted to challenge any suggestion.

- The facilitator writes everything down so the whole group can see the entire list.

When coming up with these influences, group members should focus on the practice's mission. They should look not only at their individual areas of concern but also at the larger picture. Typically, a group will come up with 20 to 50 items. The list from the Morris/Deasy/Dilday session included traffic, water, earthquake, fashion, and self-image.

Now the group is ready to develop its *critical success factors* (CSF). To do so, it should ask the question: "What must we do to accomplish our mission?" CSFs are not the *how* of the practice; they are not directly manageable. Rather, they are statements that begin with phrases such as "We must..." or "We should..." Table B.1 shows the Morris/Deasy/Dilday list.

In formulating your list of CSFs, you should use the necessary-and-sufficient rule: Each item on the list must be necessary to the mission and, taken together, the list must be sufficient to achieve the mission.

Each CSF should deal with a single issue; the word "and" is not permitted. You shouldn't have more than eight CSFs. That seems to be the limit of how many different items a management team can concentrate on continuously without losing its focus.

Initially, the group will come up with far more than eight items. You will have to work hard to reduce the number, but it is an effort that pays off. Again, the decisions on the list are made by consensus. Everyone has to agree; everyone has to buy in. Reaching agreement on the critical success factors usually takes between 2 and 3 hours. The amount of time depends on how many people are participating.

The third step in the process is to identify and list what has to be done to accomplish the CSFs. This might mean assuring design quality, aggressively developing staff, and doing a better job of managing financial resources. The group now draws up a list of business functions: the actual activities that the practice carries out in accomplishing its mission.

In preparing the list of business functions, again you will use the necessary-and-sufficient rule: Each function on the list must be necessary to achieve a CSF, and together all the functions are necessary to accomplish the mission. An example of a list of business functions for Morris/Deasy/Dilday is shown in Table B.1.

There are additional rules for the list of business functions. Each description of a function should have a verb plus an object. Each should contain only one function; the use of "and" is not permitted. Each should have an owner, the person responsible for carrying it out. The owner should be a member of the management team that agreed to the CSFs. The function should be described in such a way that you will be able to measure how well you perform it.

Table B.1. Graphing the Project

Business Functions	Skilled, motivated staff	Diverse, substantial projects	Quality design	Satisfied clients	Response to change	Financial resources	Well-managed organization	Image	Count	Quality
P1 Develop staff	x	x	x	x	x	x	x	x	8	C−
P2 Develop organization	x	x		x	x	x	x	x	7	C−
P3 Monitor the market		x			x				2	C+
P4 Monitor trends in the field		x	x	x	x				4	E
P5 Assure design quality	x	x	x	x				x	5	C
P6 Assure quality of services	x	x		x		x	x	x	6	D
P7 Monitor client satisfaction				x		x	x	x	4	E
P8 Educate clients			x	x		x			3	E
P9 Manage financial affairs	x	x		x	x	x	x	x	7	C+
P10 Market the firm		x	x			x		x	4	B
P11 Maintain quality environment	x							x	2	C

Header spanning columns: *Critical Success Factors*

Quality ratings: A = excellent; B = fair; C = poor; D = bad; E = embryonic or not at all.

SOURCE: Adapted and reprinted by permission of *Harvard Business Review*. An exhibit from "How to Make a Team Work," by Maurice Hardaker and Bryan K. Ward, November–December 1987. Copyright © 1987 by the President and Fellows of Harvard College; all rights reserved.

As a rule of thumb, you should have three or four business functions for each member of the management team. If you are the sole proprietor or the sole principal in a small office, however, you are responsible for all the functions. In such a case, keep the list to 10 to 12 functions.

Now that you have formulated the list of business functions, you must determine which are most important and which have the greatest impact on the accomplishment of your mission. To do that, list the CSFs in random order on the horizontal axis of a matrix as shown in Table B.1. List the business functions in random order on the vertical axis.

Consider the first critical success factor. Ask this question: Which business functions must be performed especially well for us to achieve this CSF? The purpose is to identify *only* the business functions essential to that CSF. If a function directly contributes to the accomplishment of the CSF, have the facilitator mark an x in the appropriate box. Continue down the list until you have evaluated each function. Then look at all the functions for a given CSF and ask whether, when taken together, they are sufficient for its achievement. If the list is not sufficient, you need to review the list of business functions to determine what else is needed. When there is agreement, proceed to the next CSF and so on through the list.

You now have a list of business functions that are necessary to accomplish each CSF. The next step is to determine which business functions you need to focus on first. At this point, you determine your priorities.

The most important business functions are those that affect the greatest number of CSFs. But you also need to know how well each function is already being performed. APM uses a subjective rating system:

A = excellent performance

B = good performance

C = fair performance

D = poor performance

E = informal or embryonic performance or not being performed at all.

The group rates each function by consensus and notes the rating in the quality column of the matrix.

You can put the information together by using a chart similar to that in Table B.2. The quality of each process is plotted horizontally, and the impact of each function is plotted vertically. The functions in the upper left in boldface type are given the highest priority because they affect

Table B.2. Selecting Priorities.

					Number of critical success impacts
		P1			8
		P2			7
		P9			
	P6				6
		P5			5
P4 P7		P10			4
P8					3
		P3 P11			2
					1
					0
E	D	C	B	A	

Quality scale

Quality ratings:
A = excellent
B = good
C = fair
D = bad
E = informal, embryonic, or not at all

SOURCE: Adapted and reprinted by permission of *Harvard Business Review*. An exhibit from "How to Make a Team Work," by Maurice Hardaker and Bryan K. Ward, November–December 1987. Copyright © 1987 by the President and Fellows of Harvard College; all rights reserved.

the greatest number of CSFs and are currently performed least well. Completing the graph is the last step in the intensive session.

The information in Tables B.1 and B.2 provides the basis for your strategic plan:

- The mission statement sets the direction for the practice.

- The critical success factors define goals for the practice over the planning period.

- The quality ratings for each function provide an assessment of your strengths and weaknesses.

- The determination of priorities for each function defines your strategies for accomplishing those goals.

The process, however, is not finished. The owners of the most important functions must analyze the performance of those functions and devise plans to improve them. These detailed plans should be presented to the group at a later date and assembled into an operational plan for the practice.

As with the comprehensive strategic planning process, APM should be repeated annually. If you have succeeded in addressing the issues, there will be a shift in the graph. The functions that are critical should be strengthened by the attention given them. Each function should show improved performance. Over time, as you improve your performance, the ratings on the graph should shift to the right. As the practice and the external environment change, new CSFs and new functions will appear. The accelerated planning method enables you to track the changes and take action.

Prospective Hindsight: A Visualization Technique

Another method of formulating your mission and goals is a visualization technique called *prospective hindsight*. It treats the future as if it were the present and the present as if it were the past. You use imagination to invent your future and work back to the present to figure out how to get there. This approach allows you to pull your strategy into the future rather than be pulled by it.

Prospective hindsight works because vivid visualization operates on the brain in a manner similar to that of actual experience. The key to this technique is to imagine your future in as much detail as possible. The more you engage your senses in visualizing the future, the more effective you will be.

To use this technique, sit in a comfortable chair in a quiet room with the lights low. Take some deep breaths. Relax. Close your eyes. When you are in a state of deep relaxation, imagine you are 5 years in the future, you are sitting in your office, and you are thinking about the time, 5 years before, when you first started planning for your practice.

Through hard work and good fortune, you have achieved or exceeded every goal you set for the practice at that time.

Describe what that office looks like. How large is it? What kind of furniture does it have? What kind of art is on the walls? What sounds do you hear as you sit at your desk? Give as many details as you can.

Now describe what you have accomplished. How large is your practice? What kinds of projects have you completed? What kinds of clients do you have? What kind of staff do you have? How are you perceived by your clients? By the public? By your colleagues? Again, be as detailed in your description as you can be.

You may take several attempts before you develop a clear picture of your desired future. Once you have a specific image, however, you can work backwards from it to determine the steps you must take to realize it. That image becomes the basis for your plan.

Bibliography

Adizes, Ichak, *Corporate Lifecycles*, Prentice Hall, Englewood Cliffs, New Jersey, 1988.

Adizes, Ichak, *How to Solve the Mismanagement Crisis*, The Adizes Institute, Santa Monica, California, 1985.

Ailes, Roger, and Jon Kraushar, *You Are the Message*, Dow Jones-Irwin, Homewood, Illinois, 1988.

Allen, Jane Elizabeth, *Beyond Time Management*, Addison-Wesley, Reading, Massachusetts, 1986.

Andrews, Kenneth R., *Concept of Corporate Strategy*, revised, Richard D. Irwin, Inc., Homewood, Illinois, 1980.

Argyris, Chris and Donald Schon, *Organizational Learning: A Theory of Action Perspective*, Addison-Wesley, Reading, Massachusetts, 1978.

Beckhard, Richard, and Reuben T. Harris, *Organizational Transitions*, 2nd ed., Addison-Wesley, Reading, Massachusetts, 1987.

Bennis, Warren, *On Becoming a Leader*, Addison-Wesley, Reading, Massachusetts, 1989.

Bennis, Warren, *Why Leaders Can't Lead*, Jossey-Bass, San Francisco, California, 1989.

Bennis, Warren and Burt Nanus, *Leaders*, Harper & Row, New York, 1985.

Block, Peter, *Flawless Consulting*, University Associates, San Diego, California, 1981.

Burley-Allen, Madelyn, *Listening*, John Wiley and Sons, New York, 1982.

Churchill, Neil C. and Virginia L. Lewis, "The Five Stages of Small Business Growth," *Harvard Business Review*, pp. 30–50, May–June 1983.

Coxe, Weld, Nina F. Hartung, Hugh Hochberg, Brian Lewis, David H. Maister, Robert F. Mattox, and Peter Piven, *Success Strategies for Design Professionals*, McGraw-Hill, New York, 1987.

Cuff, Dana, *Excellent Practice*, report to the National Endowment for the Arts, 1989.

DePree, Max, *Leadership Is an Art*, Michigan State University Press, East Lansing, Michigan, 1987.

Egan, Gerard, *Change-Agent Skills B: Managing Innovation and Change*, University Associates, San Diego, California, 1988.

Filley, Alan C., *The Compleat Manager*, Green Briar Press, Middleton, Wisconsin, 1978.

Franklin, James R., *In Search of Design Excellence*, American Institute of Architects, Washington, D.C., 1989.

Gutman, Robert, *Architectural Practice: A Critical View*, Princeton Architectural Press, Princeton, New Jersey, 1988.

Hardaker, Maurice, and Bryan K. Ward, "How to Make a Team Work," *Harvard Business Review*, pp. 112–120, November–December 1987.

Hickman, Craig R., and Michael Silva, *The Workbook for Creating Excellence*, New American Library, New York, 1986.

Hobbs, Charles R., *Your Time and Your Life: Insight System for Planning*, Nightengale-Conant Corp., Chicago, 1983. (sound cassette)

Hurst, David K., "Of Boxes, Bubbles, and Effective Management," *Harvard Business Review*, pp. 78–88, May–June 1984.

Kirkpatrick, Donald L., *How to Manage Change Effectively*, Jossey-Bass, San Francisco, California, 1985.

Koberg, Don, and Jim Bagnall, *The Universal Traveler*, revised, William Kaufmann, Inc., Los Altos, Caifornia, 1981.

Kouzes, James M. and Barry Z. Posner, *The Leadership Challenge*, Jossey-Bass, San Francisco, Caifornia, 1989.

Kriegel, Robert J. and Marilyn Harris Kriegel, *The C Zone*, Ballantine, New York, 1984.

Livingston, J. Sterling, "Pygmalion in Management," *Harvard Business Review*, pp. 121–130, September–October 1988.

Lynch, Dudley, and Paul L. Kordis, *Strategy of the Dolphin*, William Morrow, New York, 1988.

Maccoby, Michael, *Why Work*, Simon & Schuster, New York, 1988.

Maister, David H., *Professional Service Firm Management*, 4th ed., Maister Associates, Boston, 1989.

Mintzberg, Henry, *Mintzberg on Management*, The Free Press, New York, 1989.

Mintzberg, Henry, *The Nature of Managerial Work*, Harper & Row, New York, 1973.

Morgan, Gareth, *Images of Organization*, Sage Publications, Newbury Park, California, 1986.

Pascale, Richard, "The Paradox of 'Corporate Culture': Reconciling Ourselves to Socialization," *California Management Review*, pp. 26–41, Winter 1985.

Quinn, Robert E., *Beyond Rational Management*, Jossey-Bass, San Francisco, California, 1988.

Russo, J. Edward and Paul J. H. Schoemaker, *Decision Traps*, Doubleday, New York, 1989.

Schein, Edgar H., *Process Consultation*, vol. 1, 2nd ed., Addison-Wesley, Reading, Massachusetts, 1988.

Schon, Donald A., *The Reflective Practicioner*, Basic Books, New York, 1983.

Shapero, Albert, *Managing Professional People*, The Free Press, New York, 1985.

Sirkin, Harold and George Stalk, Jr., "Fix the Process, Not the Problem," *Harvard Business Review*, pp. 26–33, July–August 1990.

Smith, Peter B. and Mark F. Peterson, *Leadership, Organizations, and Culture*, Sage Publications, Newbury Park, California, 1988.

Steil, Lyman K., Joanne Summerfield, and George de Mare, *Listening*, McGraw-Hill, New York, 1983.

Steiner, George A., *Strategic Planning*, The Free Press, New York, 1979.

Vroom, Victor H. and Philip W. Yetton, *Leadership and Decision-Making*, University of Pittsburgh Press, Pittsburgh, Pennsylvania, 1973.

Wanous, John P., *Organizational Entry*, Addison-Wesley, Reading, Massachusetts, 1980.

Weinberg, Gerald, *The Secrets of Consulting*, Dorset House, New York, 1985.

Zaleznik, Abraham, *The Managerial Mystique*, Harper & Row, New York, 1989.

Index

About the Author

Norman Kaderlan, Ph.D., is principal of Kaderlan/Welch, a consulting firm in Los Angeles specializing in assisting design practices in management and marketing. He holds a doctorate in management and has twenty years experience in managing a variety of creative organizations and activities at the local, regional, and national levels. As a consultant, in addition to working with private clients, he conducts workshops and presents seminars around the country and internationally. Dr. Kaderlan is a faculty member in the Interior Design Program of UCLA Extension where he developed and now teaches a course in managing and marketing professional design services. He has taught seminars about the management and marketing of design firms and fine arts organizations at the UCLA Graduate School of Management, University of Wisconsin-Madison, University of San Francisco, and Woodbury University. Dr. Kaderlan serves as Professional Practice Editor for *L. A. Architect*.